pool search

cool search

Keeping your
organization
in touch and
on the edge...

Jean Lammiman and Michel Syrett

CAPSTONE

First published 2004 by
Capstone Publishing Limited (A Wiley Company)
The Atrium
Southern Gate
Chichester
West Sussex PO19 8SQ
http://www.wileyeurope.com

CIP catalogue records for this book are available from the British
Library and the US Library of Congress

ISBN 1-84112-430-3

Typeset in ITC Leawood 11/16pt by Sparks Computer Solutions Ltd
http://www.sparks.co.uk

Printed and bound by TJ International Ltd, Padstow, Cornwall

CONTENTS

Acknowledgements vii

PART ONE **1**
1 Cool Beginnings 3
2 The Provenance of Cool 18
3 Outside Cool 45
4 Inside Cool 92
5 Crux 132
PART TWO **159**
6 Cool Leadership 161
7 Managing Cool 180
8 Brainstorming Cool 199
9 Branding Cool 212

Summary 221
References 229
Index 235

To Thomas and Stuart,
Coolsearchers

ACKNOWLEDGEMENTS

The approach we used to research this book was a privately undertaken survey of teenagers and young adults, aged between 17 and 25, together with their parents (see example in 'The Provenance of Cool'), coupled with more extensive interviews with four families. We then cross-correlated the feedback with the wealth of literature on Millenial and Generation Y attitudes and behaviour, most of which was written during or immediately before or after 2000, to come up with a fresh perspective on the subject.

So, first of all, we want to thank all those who took part in the survey and give a special acknowledgement to those who took part in the follow-up interviews, namely:

- Thomas, Stuart and Sophie;
- Owen, Alun, Sam and Pat;
- Katya, Max and Carol;
- James, Ruth and Cec.

We will encounter their views throughout the book.

Next, we want to acknowledge the 'thinkers' on the subject whose views helped to shape our own. These are:

- Chris Anderson, *The Economist*;
- Marian Salzman, chief strategy officer of advertising agency Euro RSCG Worldwide;
- Leon Krietzman, author, *The 24 Hour Society*;
- Martin Lindstrom, author, *Brandchild*;

- Doug Petrie, writer, *Buffy the Vampire Slayer*;
- Don Tapscott, author, *Growing Up Digital*;
- Bruce Tulgan, author, *Managing Generation Y*;
- Thomas Frank, author, *The Conquest of Cool*;
- Ricardo Semler, chief executive, Semco.

Finally, we want to acknowledge everyone at home who has, over the years, put up with our scribblings, on both this and other projects, particularly T&S, Kerri, Leila, Douglas, Maggie, Zach and YB – and especially John, our personal anchorman.

Jean Lammiman and Michel Syrett

January 2004

PART ONE

COOL BEGINNINGS

I am not young enough to know everything
Oscar Wilde, Irish playwright 1854–1900

CoolSearch is about youth. The culture, not just the reality. A culture that reverses the nostrum that the older you get, the more you know. A culture that is constantly being re-defined because it is not just the under-30s that espouse it. A culture that is changing the marketplace and the work-place, not just the streets.

In the first decade of a new millennium, we are all Dorian Grays. Youth is the beautiful age that older people aspire to emulate or recover. Youth is a matter of choice, not chronology. And this is not just about 'looking young', about wearing combat trousers, working out at the gym or signing up for plastic surgery. It is about thinking young and behaving young.

In the first flush of youth culture, in the age of Presley and the Stones, we followed the Corinthian code. We dressed differently, thought differently and followed our natural instincts at school, at college, in digs, only to 'put it all away' once we entered the adult world of the parent, the professional or the office.

Now, under the pressure of a new generation that is not going to make this compromise to get on with their lives, we are taking the St Paul gospel more seriously. We are beginning to realize that we lose something vital to our-selves, and to the environment we help to shape, in letting our natural instincts be watered down by pragmatism and sober reality.

More or less at the turn of the century, the latest crop of teenagers, those born in the 1980s, entered adult life – as workers, consumers and shapers of public policy. But the reality is that they had been playing some or all of these roles for years. The average British, Australian or American child had been exposed to anything between 20,000 and 40,000 ads a year during the whole of the 1990s.[1] In the US, children aged between 4 and 12 had spent anything between $10 billion and $30 billion a year in their own right over the same period and had influenced the purchasing decisions of their parents to the tune of five times this sum.

Few children in the same societies have ever been exposed to the workings of government, business and public policy to the same extent as these 'Millennials' – and at such an early age. 'Youth engagement' was a rising trend over this period. Teenagers and young adults sat on their schools' boards of governors as elected representatives, discussed issues of public policy with government officials, at local, national and supra-national levels, and even represented their countries at the United Nations.

The inclusion of business studies in the school curriculum and the support of these studies through industrial visits, placements, secondments and traineeships meant that, even if a Millennial had not had a paid part-time job by the time they came of age, they had both a conceptual and a practical idea of what work involved. And new-age role models such as Bill Gates and Brent Hoberman meant that a surprisingly large number – thousands and, in the United States, ten of thousands – had engaged in some kind of entrepreneurial activity by the time they left college, whether it was running a pop fanzine or setting up a local school or neighbourhood website information service. Angus Friday's events organizing enterprise at medical school is a typical example[2] (see 'The Provenance of Cool').

So it was with a great deal of media fanfare and social commentary that this generation hit society as the clock ticked away towards 1 January 2000. In part, it was because of the prospect of a new dawn that always accompanies new centuries, let alone a new millennium. In what is the quintessential novel about childhood in the twentieth century, *The Go-Between*, author LP Hartley's hero writes: 'The year 1900 had an almost mythical appeal for me ... the first year of the century, winged with hope, clustered the signs of the zodiac, each somehow contriving to suggest a plenitude of life and power, each glorious, though differing from the others in glory.' New millennium, new century, new generation, new ideas, new attitudes, new outlook, new behaviour.

This is a generation to be reckoned with. They are going to overtake the country.

David Spangler,
US Director of Market Research, Levi's Jeans

In part it was because the new century coincided with the longest unbroken period of economic growth in living memory – and the fact that the Millennial generation was the largest in size since the post-war baby boom 50 years before. In the United States – where the consumer theories originated that spawned terms like baby boomers (born in the 1940s and 1950s), Generation X (born in the 1960s and 1970s) and Generation Y (born in the 1970s and 1980s) – optimism about continuing growth coincided with the fact that Generation Y was twice the size of Generation X (80 million to 44 million) and matched the numbers of baby boomers (77 million).[3]

Typical of the descriptions of the new generation at this time was this, from an article in *Fortune*, the business bible of North America, published in July 2000:[4]

Hey, boomers and Xers: Hold on to your baseball caps. There is a new generation upon us, the oldest barely out of high school, the youngest not yet born. They're not just any crop of youngsters, either. These are our own little heirs and scions: brilliant, gorgeous, practically perfect. You can brag all you want that they're chips off the old block, but they are not. They may have been smitten by Furbys and American Girl dolls and N*Sync the same way the boomers took to coonskin caps, Barbie, and the Beatles. But they were weaned on everything from the Internet and prosperity to academic pressure cookers, Columbine, working moms, and high divorce rates. They are fundamentally different in outlook and ambition from any group of kids in the past 50 to 60 years. The differences between us and them are not insignificant or academic, because the wave that is approaching is very big, nearly as big as the baby-boom generation. It is clear from talking to them that they already know they don't want to live or work the way we do.

Finally – and most significantly to the pundits – Generation Y, or Millennials as we will call them throughout this book, were the first generation that grew up with the most significant advance in technology since the Industrial Revolution – and, unlike their parents or elder siblings, they were masters of it. As the Digital Age's foremost guru Don Tapscott commented in 2000: 'For the first time in history, children are more comfortable and knowledgeable and about an innovation central to society – the Internet.'[5]

Spotlights were blazed on the relevance of anthropological studies, such as those of Margaret Meade, which claimed that in pre-figurative societies – those going through rapid technological evolution – parents have little to offer their children because their knowledge is not relevant. 'Adults don't have all the answers any more. They are not in a position to tell young people what to do,' commented Yvonne Fritzche, a researcher at Frankfurt's Psydata market research institute.[6] 'Technology is one of the reasons that the relationship between young and old is becoming a dialogue, rather than a lesson.'

The millennium also occurred at a time when dot.com mania was at its height – and with teenagers and young adults at the cutting edge. A whole new generation of Internet-savvy whiz-kids – for instance, Brent Hoberman and Martha Lane Fox of lastminute.com, and Kaljsa Leander of boo.com – had replaced 1980s business heroes such as Richard Branson, Alan Sugar and Anita Roddick (see Table 1.1).

According to an Opinion Research Council survey,[7] 54 per cent of 18- to 24-year-olds were highly interested in starting a business in 2000, compared with 36 per cent of 35- to 64-year-olds. *Vanity Fair*, the US oracle of trend spotting, coined the word 'enfantrepreneurs' to describe students at Ivy League universities that ran on-campus businesses. Top of the headlines in that year was the news that Harvard University had struck down a ban on student businesses run from dormitories.

The state of the art view about Youth Inc. at the time was summarized in a major survey on the young published in *The Economist* in its Christmas 2000 edition.[8] Author Chris Anderson pinpointed six main characteristics worth noting about the Millennial generation:

- *They welcome change.* Young adults are, by nature, well-suited to the unpredictable workplace of the future. They have less baggage and can therefore afford to take risks.

Table 1.1   UK Top 20 dot.coms in 2000

Pos[n]	Dot.com	Business	Founder(s)	Year founded	No. of staff
1	lastminute.com	late bookings	Brent Hoberman, Martha Lane Fox	1998	60
2	qxl.com	auctions	Tim Jackson	1997	n/a
3	NetCall.co.uk	callbacks	Geoffrey Rubins, John Burnett, David Rothschild	1998	39
4	icollector.com	collectibles	James Corsellis, Simon Montford	1994	54
5	gameplay.com	games	Dyan Wilk	1999	68
6	sportingbet.com	gambling	Mark Blanford, Geoffrey Wilkensen	1997	35
7	virtual partners	net security	Jason Drummond	1996	n/a
8	realcall.com	callbacks	Eric Vanderkleij, J Martin Walker	1996	8
9	boo.com	sportswear	Kaljsa Leander, Ernst Malmsten, Patrik Hedelin	1999	250
10	netbenefit.co.uk	e-solutions	Jonathan Robinson, Keith Young, Larry Bloch	1995	35
11	peoplesound.co.uk	music	Ernesto Schmitt	1998	25
12	nettec.net	net strategy	Jeremy White	1995	75
13	Internet Exchange	net cafes	Robert Proctor, Simon Henderson	1996	n/a
14	NCipher.com	encryption	Alex and Nicko von Someron	1996	45
15	orchestrastream.com	data software	Charles Muirhead	1996	48
16	WGSN.com	fashion infomediary	Julian Worth, March Worth	1998	200
17	netstore.net	data back-up	Paul Barry-Welsh, Geoff Maynard	1996	30
18	mondus.com	online tenders	Rouzbeh Pirouz, Alexander Staub	1997	20
19	equiinet.co.uk	net access	Bob Jones, John Sunners, Andrew Hurdle, Keith Baker	1998	19
20	mediasurface.com	content software	Ben Hayman, Stephen Hebditch	1996	40

Source: *Management Today Survey*, 2000, Bain & Co.

- *They think differently*. Where years of education, training and experience were once necessary to succeed, the emphasis is now on high energy, fast thinking and quick learning. Being self-taught is no longer a barrier.

- *They are independent.* Today's twentysomethings came of age as the social contract between employers and workers was dissolving. They have never expected loyalty from a company, nor have they expected to give it. They define themselves by their skills, not the firm they work for. If they have reached this point, what about the kids right behind them?

- *They are entrepreneurial.* The survey quoted Margaret Reagan, a consultant with Towers Perrin,[9] which studies workforce trends, who predicted in 1999 that barely a third of young people entering the workforce in the coming decade would take steady jobs with companies, with most opting to freelance, work under contract or take on part-time employment.

- *They want opportunity more than money and security.* They would rather take a cut in salary or work from home in poverty to build up the enterprise they want and are able to control or influence than sign up for a well-paid job that leaves them powerless.

- *They demand respect in a way their predecessors couldn't.* Or, as Bruce Tulgan, author of *Managing Generation Y*, put it: 'Dues-paying is an obsolete concept in a market that offers no hope of long-term security.'[10]

Three years is a long time in the post-industrial economic world. The dot.com crash in 2001 dampened much of the heady predictions about young entrepreneurialism dominating the business world. In any case, it is worth stressing – as we do in more detail in 'Outside Cool' – that entrepreneurial aspirations are more a characteristic of young people in America, Australia and Britain than they are in mainland Europe or Japan, where disillusion with a post-World War II social contract based on a job for life and a safe pension has not been replaced by the kind of baggage-free,

Adults don't have the answers any more. Technology is one of the reasons that the relationship between the young and old is becoming a dialogue, rather than a lesson. It affects the traditional role of authority in a way that brings generations closer together. You can't rebel against helplessness.

Yvonne Fritzche,
market researcher, Psydata

free-agent philosophy of a deregulated economy.

In any case, recent economic downturn in America and Britain has hit Millennials as hard as, or even harder than, older workers (again, see 'Outside Cool'), forcing the digital prophets to qualify their turn-of-the-decade euphoria. Bruce Tulgan was recently quoted as saying that, while Generation Y workers tend to be 'technically savvy, voracious learners, highly confident, and ambitious', they have lacked 'the feeling of vulnerability, and an understanding of the uncertainty that characterizes the real new economy' – and that consequently a recession was good for them. So parents, after all, have something to teach their kids. They may know little about technology, but they sure know how to live through rocky times.[11]

So now is a good time to re-examine the concept of the Millennial generation being baggage-free technological entrepreneurs – and to try to pick apart what characteristics attributed to them are genuinely unique or potentially world changing. In this book – by undertaking our own interviews with 18- to 25-year-olds and their parents and by re-interpreting what has been written about Millennials or Generation Y in the wake of a more sober economic outlook – we try to focus on the less sexy but undoubtedly striking attitudes of these young adults that have the capacity to overturn existing business thinking or management practice.

From this we have concluded that it is not their technological prowess that is groundbreaking but their outlook. It is not even that their general sense of corporate employment – as boring, useless and divisive – is any different from the picture we had as teenagers; it is that this impression has been reinforced, not dispelled, by negative depictions in the media over the 1990s and by first-hand feedback or second-hand impressions of their parents and elder siblings under stress during a decade when the post-World War II social contract of a job for life and a safe pension was not just questioned but blown out of the water.

Furthermore, influenced by hit television serials such as *Friends* and *Buffy The Vampire Slayer,* and the broader social bonds facilitated by Internet and mobile phone exchanges, Millennials stick together as a group far more than their Generation X predecessors, whose key characteristic was a kind of ironic detachment.

As one of the writers on the *Buffy* series, Doug Petrie (quoted in more detail in 'The Provenance of Cool') commented at the height of its popularity: 'This generation is grappling with the issue of connectedness. There's nothing singular to latch on to. The Internet, despite all these kids logging on, isn't enough. They're desperate for connection and don't find it in cold cyberspace. Ten years ago the catchphrase was "whatever", meaning "who cares?" But Buffy won't say "whatever". These are people who care passionately about each other.'[12]

This collegiateness is one of the reasons why Millennials are essential recruits at a time when innovation is a necessity, not a nice-to-have. A recent survey of nearly 400 managers by researchers at the UK's Roffey Park Management Institute[13] found that work teams that achieved the most creative output were led or

Gen-Yers picked up the free-agent mind-set, but theirs was driven by a boom mentality. While they tend to be technically savvy, voracious learners, highly confident, and ambitious, they have lacked the feeling of vulnerability, and an understanding of the uncertainty that characterizes the real new economy. This recession may be a blessing for them.

Bruce Tulgan (2001)
Managing Generation Y

heavily influenced by individuals with well-honed interpersonal and communication skills, as well as integrity, clarity of direction, and an ability to influence others and generate trust and the productivity of the team.

Other qualities included an ability to build and maintain relationships, a participative management style and good links not only within the wider organization but also with the network of stakeholders that have an interest in their output. Because anything between a half and two-thirds of all teams now have to operate at a distance, all members needed the ability to compensate for the misunderstandings that sometimes occur because the nuances of facial and body language which enhance face to face interactions are not wholly replicable by current technology.

Well, 'connectivity' has been meat and drink to Millennials since they were small children. They have networked more extensively and with a broader social group than any of their predecessors. Because they have achieved this using chat groups on the Web and mobile phone texting, they are more than used to this new medium and more capable than their parents and elder siblings of bonding with people at a distance. Moreover, they are naturally collegiate (see 'The Provenance of Cool'), loyal to their own self-made community of friends and contacts and see mutual trust as an absolute must in their private lives.

Similarly, Kristina Murrin – the managing partner of What If? a consultancy that works with big corporations such as Unilever and Bass (now owned by Six Continents) – recently stressed at a training conference organized by Britain's Chartered Institute of Personnel and Development that new 'organizational' characteristics associated with creativity are particularly prevalent among under-25s.[14]

These characteristics include 'freshness' – the ability to come up with new ideas for products or services by doing something different or seeking different stimuli – and 'realness' – the ability to keep in touch with the real world and turn ideas into reality. Both characteristics require people who have a strong link to the world outside the corporation and can interpret it through unblinkered eyes. 'There is no substitute for a stimulating life outside work and the 24/7 lifestyle of the new generation, with its emphasis on living more than one life in parallel, provides stimuli a plenty,' she stressed.

However, this mutual fit between company needs and Millennial characteristics comes at a price. Millennials are not going to demonstrate these qualities unless they are properly engaged and motivated – and this commitment and engagement has to be demonstrated at ground level. Most Millennials experimenting with corporate employment for the first time will ignore the blandishments of corporate branding and focus on the attitude and leadership qualities of the line manager in front of them. What they see, in their view, is what they are going to get.

Malcolm Higgs, professor of organizational psychology at Britain's Henley Management College, put it in management-speak when he argued forcibly in 2002 that effective front-line leadership was the only way of guaranteeing employee loyalty among well-qualified 18- to 25-year-olds: 'If [young] people are unhappy with their immediate boss then either they will leave their organization or, if they stay, they will adopt an approach that says "you can't make me leave and I will dig in." Either way, they will not put in any extra effort and you will lose commitment.'[15]

Millennial-age graduates taking part in a 2002 survey by global headhunters Kendall Tarrant Worldwide confirmed this. 'If we're rewarded and given emotional spin-offs then we'll be incredibly loyal,' said one respondent, 25-year-old Tamsin Northridge. 'It's in the employer's interest to be creative about how they use their staff. No one wants to leave a good working environment that they've helped to create.'[16]

According to Henry Huang, a 24-year-old graduate trainee at the advertising agency Rapier and another survey respondent, his generation's demands have evolved from high expectations. 'I think we've learned from the experience of our parents and we are not prepared to give up our lives for the wrong job.' Among the must-have job characteristics he cites are a non-hierarchical office, plenty of feedback and the opportunity for personal achievement.

The Millennials we interviewed for this book were blunter still. James, in the middle of an industrial placement, commented: 'I can see no reason to go the extra mile in order to increase management figures' end-of-year bonuses; if I work then it's for me. Seeing "sad" contemporaries putting ridiculous amounts of effort in for little or no extra reward also influenced my early attitudes towards work.'

'The quality of management in most companies – meaning their ability to make you want to get up in the morning raring to get to work – is piss-poor in my view,' chimes in Sam, who works for an estate agent. 'I have a boss at the moment that I want to work hard for. But it's down to him, not the company. If he were to be replaced by someone more typical, I would rather stay at home or help my boyfriend run his business.'

'So, what's new?' you might say. Haven't young people always been disaffected, seeing corporate work as boring, useless and divisive? Don't they always conform in the end?

The first hypothesis is true (see 'Outside Cool'); the second, less so. The social networks built up by most Millennials by the time they are young adults owes far less to mainstream corporate culture than those of their parents or elder siblings at the same age. A far higher proportion of these networks are likely to made up of peers who are home-based free agents, who regard old-fashioned brand image building with suspicion and whose social (as well as professional) lives do not revolve around a constant, all-encompassing workplace.

Fiercely loyal to their own, they are that much more shocked by the lack of loyalty demonstrated to each other by work colleagues in the workplaces they encounter as school or college leavers. On the receiving end of up to 20,000 commercial messages a year since childhood, they know when they are being manipulated and are that much more intolerant of cant, responding better to humour, irony and unvarnished truth.

These perceptions and outlooks, taken over time, are far more ground shaking than their affinity with the Web – important though it is. In addition to overturning contemporary HR management practice (explored in 'Inside Cool') and image-building brand management (explored 'Outside Cool') – and taken in tandem with their early exposure to, and education in, advanced public policymaking (see above) – they could fundamentally transform international corporate social policy, concepts of intellectual property ownership and international investment (see 'Crux').

Their views are increasingly going to become those of the societies in which they live – and it is this that makes us all Dorian Grays. As *The Economist*'s own survey of youth in 2000 puts it:

> *We are in the middle of a changing of the guard. The young are moving from the shadows to the spotlight in the workplace, thanks to a convergence of forces that play to youth's strength – from technology to the pace of change to the tearing down of the traditional corporate order. Why focus on the late teens and twentysomethings? Because they are the first young who are in a position to change the world, and are actually doing so.[17]*

CONCLUSIONS AND AIMS

Taking these conclusions as a starting point, this book aims to do two things. The first is to provide a stark and uncompromising depiction of the world of work and consumerism as Millennials see it. In the classic American novel, *To Kill a Mockingbird*, the hero Atticus Finch tells his daughter that the only way you are going to understand other people is to step into their shoes and walk about in them for a while. It is easy to be dismissive and patronizing about the seemingly uncompromising views teenagers and early adults take about work and the consumer society. But with this generation, for all the reasons we have described above, these views are likely to stick. Forewarned, from the view of the corporate recruiter and brand manager, is forearmed.

The second, largely dealt with in the second half of the book, is to suggest strategies that corporations can use to respond to these views. The options opened up by new technology and the move towards 24/7 living and working are there – and have been for some time. What matters is the mindset with which they are applied. Most of the managers that set the rules – even those from Generation X – were born and grew up when illusions about the post-war industrial and societal order were still rife. There are no illusions any more. Millennials are in many ways far more brutal and uncompromising about the world they are about to enter. The problem is that the adults they are coming into contact with have not realized it – and if they have, they have not fathomed that it could be good for business.

As Jonas Ridderstråle, co-author of *Funky Business*, has pointed out:

> *In the past, companies had a tendency to recruit people for skills and then train them for attitude. In the future, we're going to see them do the opposite. And the trick is to make a virtue out of what was previously seen as a demerit – their low boredom threshold.*
>
> *Like funk, they say, great companies are improvisational, with innovators everywhere, not just in R&D. They are driven by small, temporary teams of players that can be easily deployed and easily dismantled. We are getting quickly to the point where 90 per cent of the work that people do is by way of the intellect – and smart people do not want to work at business-as-usual firms.* [18]

THE PROVENANCE OF COOL 2

I'm cleaning up and moving on. Going straight and choosing life. I'm looking forward to it already. I'm going to be just like you: The job, the family, the big television, the car, the compact disc and electronic tin-opener. Good health, low cholesterol, dental insurance, mortgage, start-a-home, 3-piece suite, DIY, leisurewear, luggage, junk food, children, walks in the park, 9–5, good at golf, washing the car, choice of sweaters, family Christmas, indexed pension, tax exemption, cleaning the gutters, getting by, looking ahead to the day you die ...
Renton, closing lines from *Trainspotting* (film),
from the novel by Irvine Welsh[1]

At 21, Angus Friday already had the opportunity bug. Still at medical school in his native Grenada, he set up Limelight Promotions, an events organization business that soon stretched well beyond running college parties – so much so that Friday was contracted by the Grenada Government to develop, promote and manage the island's Carnival City Festival in August 1987. A special cultural promotional event organized by his company the following year also won high praise from the local press.

Revenues from the business served the highly useful purpose of financing Friday's medical school living expenses. It did not detract Friday from his mainstream career, however, and there was never any doubt in Friday's mind that the healthcare industry would be the focus for his business acumen.

The choice of the specific marketplace for his entrepreneurial talents was sparked in his mind by the strategy module of the MBA programme at Strathclyde Business School, which Friday signed up for soon after moving to the UK. Taught by Professor Kees van der Heijden, this was based on the 'five forces' model of market behaviour developed by Harvard's Michael Porter.

One of the conclusions was that if buyers aggregate their spending power in any industry, it creates opportunities for new sellers, who can penetrate the market far faster than if spending power is dispersed. In Friday's own words:

> *This struck a big chord with me. I had already registered that UK medical practices were forming themselves into primary care groups and that its effects on the pharmaceutical industry were likely to be immense.*
>
> *Encouraged by Professor van der Heijden, I focused on this issue in my choice of the project I needed to undertake to complete my MBA. I examined how the Scottish Development Agency had been able to use this development to attract pharmaceutical research and development funding to the west of Scotland. This provided a model that I was able to use successfully in setting up my own company.*

On moving to the UK, he achieved his goal. He launched FIZZ, a dot.com enterprise that provides general practitioners and family doctors with an on-line computer database that enables them to keep up to date with the latest medical and pharmaceutical developments. The enterprise was piloted with support from the state-run National

Health Service and has been marketed mainly though primary care groups, local associations of surgeries that have pooled their economic resources to buy services and medical back-up.

The enterprise ran into trouble in 2001. The market didn't prove as sustainable as he had hoped. But nothing deters Angus. When we last heard from him,[2] he was setting up TransAtlantic Ventures, a joint venture designed to explore how developments in advanced life sciences can help bring about new medical discoveries in very problematic disease areas such as diabetes, and cardiovascular and neurological disorders.

Angus is typical of a new generation of MBA students that chose the course not as a passport to a megabucks career in management consultancy or investment banking but to pick up the business skills to go it alone.

Sumantra Goshal, London Business School Professor of Strategy and author of *The Individualised Corporation*, argues that business has totally failed to engage Millennials in corporate work. Out of 140 students on a management course he taught in 1998, only 6 wanted anything to do with careers in large companies. It was as much to do with quality of life and relationships as with the work itself. 'Most of their parents had worked for big companies – quite a few had reached senior management level – and these guys had seen what their life was like from inside the home,' he said in an interview the following year.[3] 'Their answer was: not us, no way.'

Life criteria ten years on – after another decade of job shrinkage and pensions shortfall – extends well beyond a natural inclination towards the financial opportunities of start-up entrepreneurialism. Tom, born in the late 1970s, took a media degree at the UK's Bournemouth University and used the skills to help found a home-based website design studio. At the same time, he experimented in film production, winning The Shell Live Wire Award for entrepreneurialism for *Brown Money*, a 'short' in the style of 90s gangster classics *Pulp Fiction* and *Lock, Stock and Two Smoking Barrels*.

A final strand of activity was a band, Munkster, in which he played bass. This has proved the best of the three for Tom. It has brought the least immediate income, however, so he has given up the Web design work and moved back home in his mid-20s to give him the time and energy to make the band a success. After three years of scrimping and sparse living from his bedroom, the time and effort has paid off. Already well-established in London's independent club circuit, headlining at leading venues such as the Carling Academy (formerly the Marquee, where the Rolling Stones launched their career in the 1960s), the band are about to embark on their first UK tour, having cut two CDs and launched a single, 'Help Me Breath', into the lower end of the charts. Critics are comparing them to top groups such as Radiohead, Turin Brakes and the Red Hot Chilli Peppers.

Most of their parents had worked for big companies – quite a few had reached senior management level – and these guys had seen what their life was like from inside the home. Their answer was: not us, no way.

Professor Sumantra Goshal talking about students on his MBA programme

Tom argues that the attitude contrast between his and the post-war generation is that in his eyes there is no longer a 'safe' option against which to trade the financial risks of going his own way. People in the past would justify leaving behind early ambitions because they gained the security of a safe income that would extend beyond retirement age. Now the trade-off no longer exists. 'I do what I really want because I don't have the same excuses,' he says.

Sophie, Tom's girlfriend and contemporary, has attitudes about work and career that are fairly typical of her generation. She grew up with a view of conventional employment that was ambivalent turning negative. Work was something you were 'stuck with', a necessary evil that bought you the time to pursue other goals. Unlike Tom, who has always earned his living through self-employed activities, she has a traditional job as a fashion assistant with a leading monthly magazine. She enjoys it precisely because there is little office work, a lot of travel and constant change. 'There is always something new to experience and to learn from,' she says. 'I like the creative side of it. I'm not in it for the glamour. I'm more inclined to go shopping for my clothes in charity shops than Harvey Nicks [Harvey Nichols, a high-fashion London department store].'

Her social circle is not based on people at work but old school friends who have stuck together. Most are engaged in part-time or casual work to help fund their own artistic endeavours. Importantly, few of her girlfriends, including herself, have any immediate plans to start a family. 'It is something I hope I will eventually do but it is miles and miles away down the line.' Heavily influenced by the lyrics of Bob Dylan classics and the American 'road-tripping' novels of Celine and Kerouac that inspired them, she finds her spiritual values reflected more in her life outside work than she does in the office. 'The thing that would turn me off more than anything would be the idea that I am part of a regime.'

I do what I really want because I don't have the same excuses [as my parents].
Tom

Tom is even more uncompromising. He points to the fact that no single job would give him the flexibility to follow up simultaneously a variety of ambitions, all of them with friends from school or college. 'What is the point of putting up with the narrow restrictions of one all-encompassing job with a hazy pay-off when there are so many instant[ly available] worlds out there.'

The assumptions made by the Millennials – there is no security or expectation of loyalty to trade against their higher ambitions – is the product of a decade in which the promises of the post-war generations were torn up altogether. Goshal's argument that Millennials benefit from the inside view of business they gained from their parents extends well beyond students on postgraduate management courses.

The feedback picked up by their predecessors, those born in the 1960s or early 1970s, was that even if their parents' expectations of a job for life had been blown apart by the 1980/81 recession, they themselves could expect a measure of security during boom years.

There is always something new to experience and to learn from. I like the creative side of it. I'm not in it for the glamour.

Sophie (talking about her job as a fashion assistant)

A new round of mergers and acquisitions, coupled with the discipline of trading in a newly globalized world economy, put paid to that. The early 1990s were the years of 'lean manufacturing' and 'business process engineering'. Neither concept was intended to justify using job cutting to stay healthy in a boom market, but both were used as a fig leaf by large corporations to do so.

The US energy giant General Electric had already led the way, removing 104,000 of its 402,000 workers between 1980 and 1990, even though it faced no great crisis. Others followed. Compaq cut its workforce by 10 per cent in 1992, despite healthy returns, because it thought the computer industry was bound to stay intensely competitive. Goldman Sachs cut its workforce by 10 per cent – not once but twice – to increase productivity. Proctor & Gamble sent away

13,000 workers even though it was the best performing company in its business sector.[4]

The breakdown of any residual loyalty between company and individual was dramatic and felt immediately at home. Any Millennial entering the job market at the turn of the century would have been in their mid-teens during this period. If they were at school in the UK stockbroker belt of the Home Counties, for example, they may have picked up gossip about how detective agencies like the famous Kroll Associates were being called in by leading investment banks in the City to alert them to likely defections among key staff; that telephone conversations at work and even social chatter in public places were being secretly tapped; that meetings in conference rooms were being bugged; and the contents of computer hard disks were being examined for evidence of disloyalty; and how a high-flying fund manager called Nicola Horlick was suspended after allegations that she had tried to persuade her entire team to follow her to another bank.[5]

If that didn't filter through, then the current downturn in the finance industry will have. A recent survey by PricewaterhouseCoopers predicted tens of thousands more job cuts to come, and 2003 will go down as one of the grimmest years in memory, with brokers returning from holiday or a weekend break to find their possessions dumped in an office corridor in a bin bag. Maybe the number of people who had this indignity thrust upon them was smaller than reported, but this doesn't alter the damaging impression created. As ever, perception is reality, and the perception of ruthless uncaring employers is now front-page-headline sized.

Even if Millennials failed to pick up or take in their own parents' experiences, they cannot have failed to see the way in which disillusionment and mistrust of corporate promises was feeding into mainstream culture. The Dilbert strips, in which management-speak and corporate double-talk is the sole focus of satire, may have escaped their notice. But lying around the family home in video form or playing regularly on the channels would have been films such as *Wall Street* (1987) in which a multi-millionaire corporate raider screws his naïve protégé, shredding birthday cards and dismissing lunch as being 'for wimps'; *Jerry Maguire* (1996), in which the account manager of a leading sports agency is fired for writing a memo recommending that his company spends more time looking after its existing clients than looking around for new ones; *American Beauty* (2000), in which a put upon sales rep, at home and in the office, drops out of corporate life to live out his (largely sex- and drug-induced) fantasies; and most recently the television series *The Office* (2002), which ruthlessly pillories the way in which small-time managers affect to care about their staff but wind up using and abusing them.

Among books and films they will have watched in their own company, the message is even more explicit. In *The Simpsons* – ubiquitous viewing on both sides of the Atlantic – the father in the composite US family, Homer, is regularly portrayed as the sap that believes the fraudulent promises of his employers and fails to listen to the warnings of his more savvy kids, to his inevitable disadvantage. In the penultimate series of *Buffy the Vampire Slayer*, the demon-dusting heroine spends her 'working' hours as a burger bar cashier, complete with dubious managers, induction and training videos extolling hackneyed corporate 'missions' and 'values' and 'jobsworth' colleagues who toe the line in expectation of perks and favours.

The message is: Work Is Where You Get Screwed. Not that this is anything entirely new. Generation X, after all, was named after a book of the same name by Douglas Coupland in which the hero pursues quixotic activities rather than 'grow up' and get serious about a career.[6] The difference this time is that the messages are not being countered but actually confirmed by the feedback Millennials pick up from their parents.

Owen's story shows how important this has been in transforming the way in which Millennials see corporate employment. Both his parents followed successful professional careers in the law. His father, recently died, was a solicitor who worked for private land trusts and top legal practices. His mother is an academic lawyer who has conducted groundbreaking research in her field.

Yet Owen resisted parental pressure to go to university – largely because he rejected the conventional career ladder and professional aspirations that went with it. He set up his own carpet-fitting business, relying chiefly on work subcontracted to him by larger building companies.

His views about corporate employment closely mirror those of Tom (see above). 'From the start I wanted to work for myself rather than for a company. I worked for a few firms directly when I was younger and the money was terrible and the broader rewards not there at all. Everybody's interests and obsessions seemed to centre totally on a small circle of people at the office. Yet there was no loyalty between them at all.'

As with Tom and Sophie, Owen's impressions of corporate employment are reinforced by everyone around him. His brother Al worked for an estate agent before giving it up to work as a partner with his brother. 'I was stunned at how 40 to 50-year-old people who ought to know better would go out of their way to slag off their colleagues. It's hardly an environment where you are going to come home at the end of the day feeling good about yourself. In a big company, you always know in the back of your mind that you are replaceable.'

Owen's girlfriend Sam agrees and, most importantly, Owen's mother, Pat – while she still regrets the fact that he did not go to college – has a great deal of sympathy for his views. 'People of my age were the ones that first saw the post-war "deal" unravel,' she said. 'My parents' generation did wonderfully well out of stable employment. They all retired early. There were all these soft deals going on. They had the life of Riley and were kept by my generation in an index-linked paradise.'

Pat continued: 'By contrast, I had to work terribly hard to get where I am. The work involved constant travel and pressure at all hours of the day, as well as frequently in the evenings and at weekends. I was incredibly stressed a lot of the time and it showed at home. And, of course, both Owen and Al ended up feeling that they didn't want to wind up like me. Furthermore, Owen's impressions of the cutbacks in his father's profession during the last decade did nothing to shift this view.'

'A lot of Dad's friends really thought they had a job for life until the 90s recession scared the living daylights out of them,' he said. 'Some of them wound up mini-cabbing, using their company car, because there was nothing else they could do. No one was offering them any money. They were stuck in a way of thinking that was positively antediluvian. Even the perks they originally benefited from were being scaled down.'

From the start I wanted to work for myself rather than for a company. I worked for a few firms directly when I was younger and the money was terrible and the broader rewards not there at all. Everybody's interests and obsessions seemed to centre totally on a small circle of people at the office. Yet there was no loyalty between them at all.

Owen

The net result is that Owen is determined to owe nothing to anyone. Unlike Tom, he is extremely money-minded, but he shares an equally cynical view about the 'securities' of conventional employment: 'Shall I tell you why I don't think pensions any more? Because I can't actually see myself stopping working. I am not going to stop working until I am physically unable to do it any more. At 65, I will be doing what I am doing now. I accept that. I am happy to make this trade-off. At least this way I am not dependent on someone else's dicky promises.'

People of my age were the ones that first saw the post-war 'deal' unravel. My parents' generation did wonderfully well out of stable employment. They all retired early. There were all these soft deals going on. They had the life of Riley and were kept by my generation in an index-linked paradise.

Pat

Even Millennials who take a less jaundiced view of conventional employment than Owen are less prepared for what it will involve than their counterparts in previous generations. Since the early 1980s, anything between a third and a half of the total workforce in Western economies work either part-time or from home. This is increasingly the case with men as much as women. The conventional role models that shaped perceptions and attitudes to work during the highly formative early teen years are no longer in place – with the result that the first exposure to regular employment is more of a culture shock.

'I can't say that I had any preconceptions about work,' said Katya, 20, who lives at home with her mother Carol, a separated parent, and her 17-year-old brother Max. 'Mum works for herself from home. The only images of what work was like in an office were from what you saw on the TV that painted a pretty horrid picture. Like advertisements for fast-working cough medicine or flu remedies for people too scared to stay away from the office for long because they might lose out.'

The first coherent picture her brother Max had of office work was a formal placement arranged by the school. 'It was the worst two weeks of my life,' said Max. Asked why, it became clear that nothing in his life to date had prepared him for the regularity of office routine. 'At school, you spend your day moving from one class to another and being taught different subjects. In this office, there was a rigid schedule that was the same all the time.'

I was stunned at how 40- to 50-year-old-people who ought to know better would go out of their way to slag off their colleagues. It's hardly an environment where you are going to come home at the end of the day feeling good about yourself. In a big company, you always know in the back of your mind that you are replaceable.

Al

MILLENNIALS AND THEIR ATTITUDE TO WORK

Most of the opinions about work expressed in this book were based on a series of interviews we conducted with 18- to 25-year-olds (and their parents) who have entered, or are about to enter, the workforce. The feedback we received emphasized the strong influence that shifting family-based attitudes and media coverage about job security and the post-World War II social contract have had on Millennial-age workers.

Here is a typical example. The questions we posed are those we also used in other interviews.

What were your earliest perceptions of what 'work' was like and at what age?

Tidying room/cleaning basin every Saturday, aged approximately eight. This was something that I had to do, otherwise I'd be in deep, deep trouble (for an eight-year-old anyway).

Were these perceptions largely negative or positive? How did they develop over time?

Extremely negative initially – I would do almost anything to get out of doing it. As time went on I began to view 'work' as a necessary evil, and eventually it just became a routine. However, the bare minimum of effort was still put in.

This still applies for work I find tedious or feel is unnecessary, although I will engage wholeheartedly in a task I enjoy/can see the relevance of. Seeing both parents returning from work very tired (and more often than not in a bad mood due to inept colleagues/inter-departmental in-fighting and political wrangling) each weekday also put me off rather.

What helped to shape your attitudes? For example: Feedback from your parents? Depictions of work in ads, films or on television? Reading about work in magazines or papers? Conversations with friends?

School was a major factor. Depictions of work in TV programmes – e.g. *Men Behaving Badly* or *Friends* – were also important. Both these factors helped to reinforce the idea that doing anything above the bare minimum is usually a waste of time. Through these media I saw 'cool' people not working hard, and was influenced by this. I found that this 'laziness' was also a handy way to annoy parents/teachers/authority figures relatively easily...

Politically minded films/documentaries my parents regularly watch such as *The Full Monty* or *Brassed Off* helped to shape a cynical (and also self-centred) attitude towards work

– I can see no reason to go the extra mile in order to increase management figures' end-of-year bonuses; if I work then it's for me. Conversations with friends (who watched the same TV programmes and shared fairly similar interests) reinforced these views, as we all tended to agree with each other.

Seeing 'sad' contemporaries putting ridiculous amounts of effort in for little or no extra reward also influenced my early attitudes towards work.

What early work experiences, if any, helped shape your attitudes? Did you, for example, take on any school-based industrial placements or have Saturday or part-time jobs? Were these good or bad experiences?

My attitudes began to change subtly after actually gaining work experience. The core views remain largely unchanged, but I will now work much harder – even on jobs/projects I hate – in order to get the grades/promotions so that I will never have to do these jobs ever again! However, if I can see no potential for advancement then I still won't put in anything above minimum effort ...

These views were mainly formed during summer work after my first year at university – doing a job that started off as interesting, but soon became extremely repetitive and unrewarding when it became apparent that I would be doing pretty much exactly the same thing, day in, day out.

They're now being cemented by the job I'm in at the moment (still student summer work), where I can see the point of what I'm doing – even though I don't enjoy all of it – and can see a tangible goal to work towards.

What expectations do you have of work? Secure employment? Frequent job changes? Long-term financial security (e.g. a pension) or self-made opportunities? How do these link into other life aspirations – owning your own property, getting married and so on?

I would like secure employment, though I see frequent job changes as being more likely in today's climate. I'll work because I have to – in order to one day own a house, support future family and be able to pursue activities I enjoy: such as socializing (i.e. working to buy beer ...) sport, active pursuits and travel. If I were to suddenly win the lottery then I'd be off to buy a yacht and sail away to the Caribbean like a shot, unless I enjoyed the job so much that I'd do it for nothing; I view this as unlikely ...

Do your early impressions of employment in your present position match your previous perceptions of what work would be like for you?

Most of my early expectations have been matched, although I'm less cynical than usual about my current job for reasons already discussed. The only major thing that I hadn't thought would be quite so important is the social status that jobs provide, whether you like it or not. Previously I'd imagined that the only things that would matter are whether you actually *have* a job or not.

People who do would then be rated on how much they earn. I hadn't bargained for the 'Oh you hate *your* job then? I love *my* job so much; let me tell you how trusted and respected I am...' Hint: 'I am so much better than you, ha ha ha.' Everyone my age seems to brag about their jobs like this (including myself unfortunately), irrespective of whether a word they're saying is actually true or not.

I think it's because most of the people my age are in student summer placements earning very little money, so have to go on about 'job satisfaction' instead. None of the people my age I know who didn't go to university and have therefore been in full-time employment for roughly three years or more seem to do this.

ICONS AND ICONOLOGY

The Masters of the Universe were a set of lurid, rapacious plastic dolls that his otherwise perfect daughter liked to play with. They looked like Norse Gods who lifted weights, and they had names such as Dracon, Ahor, Mangelred, and Blutong. They were unusually vulgar, even for plastic toys. Yet one fine day, in a fit of euphoria, after he had picked up the telephone and taken an order for zero-coupon bonds that had brought him a $50,000 commission, just like that, this very phrase had bubbled up into his brain. On Wall Street, he and a few others – how many? – three hundred, four hundred, five hundred? – had become precisely that ...Masters of the Universe. There was ... no limit whatsoever!

Naturally, he had never so much as whispered this phrase to a living soul. He was no fool. Yet he could not get it out of his head.

Tom Wolfe, *The Bonfire of the Vanities*[7]

Millennials have their own iconography and – as we will see in the next chapter – it is radically different to the one they will encounter in the workplace.

First, it is founded on *the ability to shape your own worlds*. The iconography of the baby boomers and Generation X was shaped by alternative worlds. *Lord of the Rings*, *Dune* and *Star Wars* were all underpinned by an invented culture and mythology that is every bit as complex and deep-rooted as our own. The worlds they described and the people who populated them had their own heroes, myths, language, hierarchies and realities and these worlds populated the minds and informed the imaginations of adherents long into their adult lives.

But, critically, they were worlds created and shaped by someone else. People could envisage these worlds differently in their heads but the basic chronology was set in stone. One of the greatest challenges facing director Peter Jackson in turning *Lord of the Rings* into a film trilogy was creating a 'look' that conformed as closely as possible to the image that fanatically loyal Tolkien addicts had in their heads. He succeeded by turning to the original artwork used to illustrate the books over three generations and distilling the common elements.

Visual referencing of this kind has been at the heart of all successful science fiction and sword and sorcery mythology. The success of the sci-fi *Alien* film trilogy lay as much in director Ridley Scott's groundbreaking set designs, created in collaboration with Swiss graphic artist H.R. Giger, whose work in his own magazine *Ecronicon* had 'informed' the imagination of a whole generation of sci-fi fans, as his ability to translate the script of alternative sci-fi freaks Dan O' Bannon and Ron Cobb.

The medium of the computer game, however, has allowed Millennials a far greater capacity to shape and play with the fictional worlds that inhabit their heads. In the worlds created by computer games, there is no script. What happens is shaped by the individual playing the game. The visual imagery may well be lifted from previous predetermined fictional universes but the plot is in the head of the player.

The Tomb Raider game is typical. The designers lifted wholesale the imagery and iconography created by the popular *Indiana Jones* film series but there is nothing remotely archaeological about the heroine Lara. More importantly, each adventure she experiences is different according to who is working the software. The boundaries of imagination, and with it the sense of what is possible, has been pushed well beyond what would have been possible even ten years ago.

This level of control has been reflected in, and fuelled by, new branding strategies adopted by companies that deliberately target 'tweenagers' (8- to 14-year-olds). In his book *Brandchild*, which charts the relationships to brands, psychologist Martin Lindstrom (see 'Crux') argues that tweens' relationship to brands is fundamentally different from that of their parents.[8]

'We were brought up on passive media, but a whole new generation is completely interactive', says Lindstrom, who believes that the ad industry has miserably failed to respond to the implications. 'Interactivity is as big as TV.'

To communicate immediately with the new generation, he says, advertising will have to learn to fuse all the senses into the brand message: sound, sight, touch, smell, taste. Some companies use one or other of these – the smell of bread in supermarkets, the snap, crackle and pop of breakfast cereals – but brand-building needs to appeal to all of them, according to Lindstrom.

An interactive Web community launched in 2001, NeoPets.com, gives a good idea of what is already possible, both in terms of interactive technology and fantasy creation and in terms of outright manipulation. NeoPets is able to integrate advertisers' products and messages into the activities and adventures of the site. Users at NeoPets.com interact directly with sponsors' products, characters and messages for extended periods of time – ensuring lasting impressions.

According to PC Data Online, NeoPets.com's more than 4 million registered members spend an average of nearly six hours a month interacting with the site. And by customizing campaigns in order to meet each advertiser's needs, NeoPets.com has demonstrated strong numbers of impressions and time statistics for their sponsors, exceeding expectations by as much as fourfold.

'This form of "advertising" creates a lasting impression with our users, particularly so when compared to traditional magazine or TV ads (which may never be seen), or distracting banner ads that are frequently not even within the focus of the user,' said Lee Borth, chief operating officer with NeoPets. 'Because of the size of the site and the number of unique users aged nine to nineteen, the opportunities with this form of advertising are unlimited.'[9]

NeoPets.com is an interactive Web community where members create their NeoPet, and then select its name, colour and traits such as personality, intelligence and special abilities. With their NeoPets, Millennial-age members enter Neopia, the virtual world of NeoPets.com, which contains forests, mountains, rivers and villages – each offering unique multi-layered activities.

Members are constantly involved with the site, creating their own virtual activities, including commerce, entertainment and interaction with other members. Members can earn Neopoints, the free currency of the site, which enables them to buy virtual items in various shops, feed and care for their pet, participate in virtual auctions, and even play the stock market.

The fact that the Tomb Raider's hero Lara is a woman is not a coincidence. In baby boomer mythology, such as that in *Lord of the Rings*, the world is led by men, with women playing a largely passive role. In Generation X mythology, such as *Alien*, where women succeed, they do so in a world created by men by outclassing them at their own game. In Millennial mythology, and more importantly iconography, *there is a feminine take* on things. Visually, there is nothing masculine about Lara. Her feminine assets are in your face. Anatomically, her designers concede, a real Lara would not be able to stand up. But this is femininity for its own sake, not just a source of sexual gratification for teenage boys. Lara is *freestanding*. She *goes her own way*, in the same way as Buffy does in *Buffy the Vampire Slayer.* Her sexuality is a symbol of her own enfranchisement, a source of fulfilment for her own sex. It does not need to be compromised or played down.

Being freestanding does not, however, mean being self-centred. A heavy emphasis of the iconography of Millennial culture is *loyalty to your own*. In the opening credits of *Buffy the Vampire Slayer*, it is not Buffy alone who strides forward to dust the demons but her friends as well. Unlike the superheroes of the past, she is dependent on the support of her own self-made community – the dynamics of which reflect in every way the mutual dependence of relationships forged at school and college. This is, of course, the underlying rationale behind the enduring success of the TV series *Friends*, but it also underpins the imagery of almost all Millennial icons. Thus Tom (see above) has chosen 'career' options that enable him to work and live with his friends. This takes first place in his list of priorities – before advancement, money or security.

Jane Buckingham, head of Youth Intelligence in New York and the leader of two focus groups that US business journal *Fortune* sponsored in Los Angeles in 2000, says the

This generation is grappling with the issue of connectedness. The Internet isn't enough ... Ten years ago, the catchphrase was 'whatever', meaning 'who cares'. But Buffy won't say 'whatever'. These are people who care passionately about each other.
Doug Petrie, writer on
Buffy the Vampire Slayer

Millennials' strong friendships put them in sharp contrast to Generation X, whose disillusionment with stagnant careers has turned many of them into loner, suffering, poet-at-the-picnic types. The difference is already showing up in advertising. 'Ads aimed at Gen Xers show them living so literary, miserable-but-interesting lives,' says Buckingham. 'That approach doesn't work with the next generation. Belonging to a group is so important that I caution anyone advertising to this generation against putting a lone individual in an ad.'[10]

Doug Petrie, a writer for *Buffy the Vampire Slayer*, says there is a conscious effort to show Buffy with a loyal, tight-knit group that helps her battle demons. 'The ironic detachment that seemed to work for TV shows geared to Gen Xers doesn't work with the newest crop of kids,' says Petrie. 'Ten years ago the catchphrase was "whatever", meaning "who cares". But Buffy won't say "whatever". These are people who care passionately about each other.'[11] Adults as rescuers are deliberately excluded from Buffy too. 'Kids feel that grown-ups can't help them,' Petrie continues. 'Thirty years ago this show would have been called *Father Knows Vampires Best*. But not now.'

LANGUAGE

The yuppies had kneaded [the script] and kneaded it until it became, as Grady Rabinowitz used to say, a piece of shit. It went flatline at Warners.
Julia Phillips (1991) *You'll Never Eat Lunch in This Town Again*, p. 542

Millennial iconography is rooted in a vivid use of language. The formative teenage years of Millennials have seen a revolution in both English language content and usage. *The Oxford Dictionary* recognized this early on by launching *The Oxford Dictionary of New Words* in 1991, which now covers over two thousand words generated by politics, sports, business and Net-based technology.[12]

From sport comes rotisserie league (a parlour game in which participants create imaginary teams by 'buying' actual players and scoring points according to their real performances – named after the Manhattan restaurant La Rotisserie, where it was invented). From politics we get political correctness, clear blue water and ethnic cleansing. From fluctuating social and sexual tensions come words like sex-positive (someone who rejoices in giving into their sexual instincts and desires), riot girl (a young militant feminist), lipstick lesbian (glamorous, fashion-conscious lesbian), saddo (new word for nerd), fundie (diminutive for fundamentalist) and to flatline (as in to die). Or how about to schlomp (hang around), spooky (weird in a positive way) or smokin (updated word for live wire)?

Most importantly, from the point of view of the Millennials, we have acquired words from Internet use: mouse potato (person who spends excessive amounts of time online), otaku (Japanese version of mouse potato), hot button (the issue that prompts people to make a consumer, political or social choice), morphing (transforming one image to another digitally), netizen (member of a computer network), eyephone (virtual reality headset) and clipper chip (a digital key that allows law enforcement agencies to hack into encryption systems).

The Oxford Dictionary of New Words unleashed an unstoppable craze for charting new vocabulary. The latest *Collins English Dictionary* included such words and phrases as Billy-no-mates (a person with no friends), ladyboy (a transvestite or transsexual, especially from the Far East) and even starfucker (a person who seeks sexual relations with celebrities). 'Everything goes in,' commented Jeremy Butterfield. 'We don't like to keep words out because they reflect how people are talking and what they are saying – no matter how crude some might be.' Yet when rival dictionary *Chambers* went one further and started including phrases drawn from the latest films and videos – such as 'ya, baby' and 'shagtastic' from the hit movie series *Austin Powers* – the two companies engaged in a war of words over where or whether a line should be drawn on this 'anything goes' wordfest.

Use of vocabulary is very like use of technology. If you grow up during a period when the rules are being thrown away, you will show no constraint in experimenting. Among the words that have emerged from youth culture most recently are handbag music (catchy but naff dance music), rad (new word for cool), mosh (dancing violently, the successor to headbanging) hardcore (hard, expressionist music, the successor to punk) and dissing (putting someone down as in 'On TV, one of the Geto boys justified dissing women because "in my hood, all the women are prostitutes"' – *The Face*).[13]

This is nothing new in itself. In France and Japan particularly, underground or anti-establishment language that shifts and ebbs continuously and defines the speaker as a member of a specific generation has been a feature of youth culture since the 1960s. The difference, as with so many other facets of twenty-first-century Dorian Gray society, is that it is no longer being abandoned at the entrance door to the office, conference centre, shopping mall, trading floor or even boardroom.

In a broader social context, this language has lost none of its vigour. Three aspects are particularly relevant in its application at work and in marketing or strategy development. First, *it is highly fashionable*. You use it one year and ditch it the next. In the early 1990s, virtual reality was the cutting edge of language. 'Eyephone' and 'dataglove' both date from this period and their use was fuelled further by the release of films such as *The Lawnmower Man* (in which a mentally backward odd-job boy is turned into a psychotic genius by the use of virtual reality technology) and *Dangerous Consent* (in which the central plot turns around the development of new virtual reality software). Now, virtual reality and all its associated vocabulary and imagery are dead and gone. Similarly 'smokin' was invented in the Jim Carrey film *The Mask* and was ubiquitous for a year – but it is barely heard on the streets today.

Second, *it takes its lead from popular culture*. To flatline – used as a substitute for die or become unproductive or ineffectual – was confined to medical circles until the science fiction writer William Gibson used it in his novel *Neuromancer* ('He flatlined on his EEG ... boy I was daid'). However, it was in 1990 with the release of the film *Flatliners* – in which a group of students dangerously exploit their ability to control the moment of death before being revived – that the verb, and its noun derivative flatliner, entered the popular language. Use in relation to actual death has not become widespread but the verb in its extended form has become ubiquitous among stock market traders, marketers and pundits, to whit: 'The Ronzer had been flatlined for years. Overload on those antique circuits';[14] 'Not that it was a bad magazine, but it was a fiscal flatliner, with one of Brown's early issues just carrying 14 pages of ads'.[15]

Third, *it enlivens or reinvents itself by prefixing and juxtaposition*. Back in the 1970s, French students would enliven staid words by adding the prefix 'archi' or 'extra', as in 'archi-bien' or 'extra-nu'. Now, the scripts of Millennial and Dorian Gray programmes such as *The Simpsons* and *Buffy the Vampire Slayer* are peppered with nouns like 'trauma girl' (as in 'She is probably still a bit trauma girl about Angel right now'), 'ground-his-bones-into-dust kinda-dead' and 'dusting fashion consultant-boys'. In the weeks leading up to the 2003 Gulf War, French diplomats were dismissed by Homer Simpson as 'cheese-eating surrender monkeys'. The description was taken up nationwide by pro-war advocates.

THE AHA IN THE HA HA

> 'She grew on him like she was a colony of E. coli and he was British beef at room temperature.'
> 'It hurt the way your tongue hurts after you accidentally staple it to the wall.'
> 'He was as lame as a duck. Not the metaphorical lame duck either but a real duck that was actually lame. Maybe from stepping on a landmine or something.'
> Extracts from UK English exam essays, 2003

Playful and experimental use of language is also linked to another characteristic of Millennial culture – humour. Comedy was a key cultural medium of the 1990s. It wasn't just that the decade saw a renaissance in US comedy with a string of hits that exported well to other parts of the world, such as *Frazier*, *Cheers* and *Seinfeld*. It wasn't just that sharp-wit humour underpins most of the television or films that appealed to Millennials in their teenage years, including those not 'labelled' as comedies such as *Pulp Fiction* or *Lock, Stock and Two Smoking Barrels*.

Comedy became hip club territory. Thanks to the lead taken by Billy Connolly and Eddie Izzard, stand-up acts moved from being seen as the territory of saddos to something you clubbed out for in the same way as you went to a gig. In literal terms, it *became* a gig. Comedy clubs such as Jongleurs and the Comedy Store mirrored music venues like the Hard Rock Café in opening not only in leading North American and European centres but also on the hippy and expatriate trail in urban centres in Asia.

In the process, a new, highly globalized form of anti-establishment humour emerged – humour that genuinely crossed boundaries. For example, a highly successful comic act doing the international rounds in the late 1990s was 'How to be an Iranian' by BBC New Comedy Award winner Shappi Khorsandi and her brother Peyvand. Based on their experiences growing up in the England of Margaret Thatcher and the Iran of Ayatolla Khomeni, it was performed in venues as wide apart as Los Angeles, London and Bangkok in a mixture of English and Farsi. One of the more interesting things to emerge from its popularity was that Iran had a strong stand-up comedy tradition.

It is worth mentioning at this point that humour is the gateway to creativity. The ability to understand and produce humour requires the complex interplay of several thought processes: working memory (holding a piece of information in mind while you manipulate it); cognitive shifting (looking at a situation in different ways or from different perspectives) and abstract thinking.

Research at the University of Toronto links the ability to laugh at the complex analogies and ironies of an Eddie Izzard monologue or a comic exchange in *Friends* with the frontal lobe of the brain. 'The frontal lobe is important because it is the part of the brain that gets the most information from the rest of the brain,' explains Toronto's Professor

Prathiba Shammi. 'It brings together information from the thinking part of the brain with the emotional part of the brain.'

SUMMARY

Millennials – the generation born in the 80s that are now coming into the labour market – spent their formative teen-age years in societies where post-war verities were being not just questioned but ripped apart.

Examining the formative influences they were most likely to have been exposed to, they are entering employment with the following cultural make-up:

- A strong sense of corporate employment as senseless, hypocritical and boring.
- An iconography that stresses a feminine take on society, loyalty to your own self-made community and the ability to be freestanding and shape your own worlds.
- A perspective on the world, shaped by increasingly cross-cultural influences, that is multi-ethnic and global.
- A wholly iconoclastic and irreverent use of language, marked by humour and vivid imagery.
- A set of expectations in which there are no longer any benefits in playing safe.

As we will demonstrate in the following chapters, all of these characteristics are transforming the way businesses recruit, retain and intellectually engage Millennials in fields as diverse as personnel management, brand marketing and image-building and corporate social policy.

OUTSIDE COOL

3

If you can't beat 'em, absorb them.
'Who Built America?' American Social History
Project 1966

Of course, we have seen all of this before. The search
for cool is hardly new. In his book *The Conquest of Cool*,[1]
Washington Post business correspondent Thomas Frank
describes how the US 1960s counterculture took over
Madison Avenue advertising account managers – providing a perfect prototype for turn of the century cool 'hunters'
and, through their output, a Dorian Gray society in which
youth lifestyle is an aspiration for everyone.

As he puts it: 'Rebel youth culture remains the cultural
mode of the corporate moment, used to promote not only
specific products but the general idea of life in the cyber-
revolution. Commercial fantasies of rebellion, liberation,
and outright "revolution" against the stultifying demands of
mass society are commonplace almost to the point of invis-
ibility in advertising, movies and television programming.'

The form this took in the 1960s was slightly different.
It was the age of the slogan rather than the brand. Frank
cites the example of an advertisement for Dexter shoes that
ran in *Men's Wear* in March 1966, which pictured a number
of rather plain slip-on shoes perched on a spherical bomb
with a lit fuse. The shoes are touted as 'Dynamic, revolutionary, explosive. An entirely fresh concept in men's casu-

als that in every way captures the aggressive, independent mood and spirit of '66.'

But the assumption behind the slogans – hedonistic free-thinking youngsters are the perfect consumer model in an age of rule breaking, far out in front of their backward-looking elders or, as adman and youth specialist Merle Steir put it in 1967, 'Youth wants to see it and tell it as it is' – remains as constant and enduring in the brand-building exercises of the late 1990s. Nike shoes sold to the accompaniment of words delivered by William S. Burroughs and songs by Gil Scott Heron. Peace symbols decorated a line of cigarettes manufactured by R.J. Reynolds and the walls and windows of Starbucks coffee shops. The products of Apple, IBM and Microsoft were, and are, touted as devices of liberation.

Merle Steir himself was the prototype for the 90s cool hunter. It was he who first touted the decade's favourite statistic: that half the US population was, or soon would be, under the age of 25; and its corollary, that young people had control of some $13 billion in discretionary dollars – $25 billion if the entire age span from 13 to 22 was counted.

More than any other commentator of his era, Steir pioneered the idea that young people, in addition, were economically powerful beyond their immediate means. They had become by the late 1960s the decade's arbiters of taste, and advertising could target adults through appeals to their children. His firm, Youth Concepts, promised to unlock the mysteries of youth culture for the advertising world, organizing proto-counterculture exhibitions and, through conferences and workshops, touting

Youth wants to see and tell it as it is – adults see it as it was.
Merle Steir, adman and youth expert, 1966

the message 'You can't communicate to people you're against'.

Forty years on, cool hunting has become more sophisticated, its message aimed not only at companies who want to target newly emergent Millennials but also wannabe-cool adults among the boomer and Generation X cadres. Steir's counterpart in the first decade of the new century is 'Queen of Cool' Marian Salzman, chief strategy officer of the world's fifth largest advertising agency, Euro RSCG Worldwide – whose trend-spotting skills have made billions for clients such as Volvo, Pentel and L'Oréal.

Among her recent achievements was spotting the spending power of single professional women – 'Everyone thought they were sad spinsters; statistics proved they were happier than their married counterparts' – before the Bridget Jones phenomenon proved the point in spades. Other Salzman coups included inventing the term 'wiggers' for young whites imitating blacks, 'hottie' to describe the powerful and successful middle-aged women who have replaced trophy twentysomethings as the ultimate partners of choice for businessmen, and 'metrosexual' to describe, as she puts it, 'heterosexual urban men who enjoy fashion and back waxing but increasingly feel they are being treated as buffoons' – a category in which she includes Bill Clinton (strangely, given metrosexual's need to commit – see below), footballer David Beckham and Richard Madeley from the UK daytime chat show *Richard and Judy*.

Salzman cool hunts using a combination of statistical number crunching, peering into other women's baskets in supermarkets, reading chicklit novels and feedback from the 1300 trend-spotters she employs worldwide who email her whenever they spot something new. Two of the latest trends identified by this last source include the fact that in the economic backlash to the heady 90s, paying in cash denotes more substance and status than using a credit card; and that being overweight is no longer the anorexic-generating source of shame that it once was among teen-age girls and young women. 'Oversizing' it seems, much to Salzman's own disgust, is 'in' (at least at the time this book was written – it may be 'out' now).

Cool hunting as a profession has been around for well over a decade – and its dynamics and limitations have been delineated accordingly. It is about *now* – spotting emerging trends sufficiently early for companies to make commercial use of it because once that trend is fully out in the open it is no longer 'cool'. There is a frenzied self-fuelling vicious circle about this kind of 'diffusion research'. As Malcolm Gladwell, the *New Yorker* staff writer who wrote *The Tipping Point: How Little Things Can Make a Big Difference*,[2] explains: 'The faster everyone adopts the idea, the faster the "cool" person has to run in the opposite direction. Cool people have short attention spans and crave sensation.'

This creates a very narrow window of success because the trick of the game is not to 'create' the trend. Marian Salzman stresses that trends these days are bottom-up not top-down and any company seeking to second guess the process invariably gets it wrong. Nor is it to sell the results to the people who did create it – self-evidently, they are not going to be interested. It is to sell it to everyone else before the fact that it is no longer 'cool' in the eyes of the trendset-ters renders it 'history'.

Malcolm Gladwell cites the example of Dee Dee Gor-don, cool hunting adviser to the fashion house Converse in the 1990s, who started to observe a lot of Hispanic kids on Venice beach wearing old-fashioned shower sandals – a 'retro' homage to the 1950s fuelled by the fashion style adopted by pop sensations of the moment the Beastie Boys. She persuaded Converse to produce a copycat version of the shower sandal called the Skateboard Shoe, which made a financial killing for the company in 1995. But the shoe wasn't targeted at Venice beach Hispanics. It was targeted at wannabe Venice beach Hispanics of any ethnic background in Salt Lake City, Pittsburgh and Richmond, Virginia. The fad lasted precisely eighteen months. Other manufacturers jumped in on the act. But Converse got there first.

The faster everyone adopts the [cool] idea, the faster the 'cool' person has to run in the opposite direction.

Malcolm Gladwell, author of *The Tipping Point: How Little Things Can Make a Big Difference*

Wannabe Venice beach Hispanics, of course, come in all ages and shapes these days – and there lies the second complicating factor. Old-fashioned statistical analysis is less of a reliable indicator of future trends in a Dorian Gray society. Martin Hayward, chairman of long-established and well-respected UK market research forecasters the Henley Centre, commented in 2002:[3]

> *It used to be easy to predict what somebody's lifestyle would be by looking at the demographics. Young people were interested in fashion. Old people weren't. Men did one thing, women another. Markets were easy to segment and it was a nice, easy, tidy world. But what has happened over the past decade is that people are no longer acting their age. This means that the process of targeting consumers is different to what it used to be. Marketers are finding they have to target across much more attitudinal lines instead of age.*

But cool hunting, at best, only scrapes the tip of the iceberg when it comes to charting the new attitudes provoked by the Millennial generation. One strand – that represented by Dee Dee Gordon – does not focus on personality at all. In a recent interview, she stressed that cool hunting does not attempt to understand the person. Rather, it tries to identify taste.

The other strand – represented by Marian Salzman – does focus on personality but presents little more than a snapshot of a given category of person at a given moment in time. The term 'metrosexual', for example, focuses largely on the attitudes of a highly cosmopolitan minority of males towards their own sexuality and lifestyle. The key denominators are that while they are highly fashion conscious, they are also insecure about their own status in pop culture now dominated by aggressive female values and that, probably as a consequence, many of them look for emotional depth in meaningful relationships rather than sexual hedonism.

The emphasis here is on lifestyle choices and how this will translate into their attitudes and behaviour as consumers – the issues that are of most interest to Salzman's clients at Euro RSCG. The approach, which is largely based on observation, is less helpful in determining, for instance, how they will vote, perform at work or develop in older age.

Although the methods are much more sophisticated than those used by Merle Steir in the 1960s, the rationale is the same. Spot upcoming trends and changes in taste and style by 'chasing intellect'. Observe (rather than seek to influence) the habits of a small number of social trendsetters in media-sensitive industries such as fashion, film, recreation and music. Develop products, toys or fashion items that ride the crest of this wave. The key phrases here are 'diffusion research' (i.e. something that spreads rapidly

Over the past decade, people are no longer acting their age. This means that the process of targeting consumers is different to what it used to be. Martin Hayward, Chairman of the Henley Centre (leading UK market researchers)

across the surface), 'social contagiousness' and 'epidemic markets'.

All of these terms presuppose that the forces that influence consumer, career or lifestyle choices build up to a point where they 'tip' over into contagion or epidemic form – hence Malcolm Gladwell's choice of *The Tipping Point* for his book – only to then dissipate, rather than determining these choices consistently over time.

Long-term incremental changes are not part of the cool hunter's agenda. So it is worth taking a step back and examining a number of key characteristics of Millennials that might determine their key decisions over years and decades rather than months or weeks. We will attempt to do this by grouping these characteristics under a number of deliberately generic phrases – 'intimacy', 'loyalty', 'awareness', 'flexibility' and 'risk' – that may not apply to all young adults born after 1977 but that certainly characterize them as a group.

INTIMACY

> *The online self is supported by neither time, space nor body, and yet it is unmistakably present.*
>
> From a Mintel website

Internet and mobile phone technology is in the process of transforming not only the way developed societies communicate with each other but also how we develop intimate relationships. Boomers have encountered and adjusted to it in middle age. Generation X encountered and adjusted to it in late teens and early 20s. Millennials are the first generation to have grown up with it from early childhood.

The long-term legacy is likely to be profound. As Malcolm Gladwell argues in *The Tipping Point*, the way adults form and sustain relationships – as employees and consumers as well as with friends and lovers – stems largely from the way they did it in school. For most of the twentieth century, teenagers in developed countries interacted with their friends at school and on returning home played with people in their neighbourhood. The universe of the average teenager was therefore shaped by the length of the school day, together with the school's catchment area and the perspective of the people who lived in it.

The advent of the second household phone in the 1960s revolutionized the teenager's ability to sustain and extend the scope of their existing relationships but did little to broaden their universe or alter the way they were initiated. You met friends or potential dates in the same places – the schoolyard, the local clubhouse or community centre – and then indicated your willingness to carry it forward (or not) by exchanging telephone numbers.

Surfing the Web and texting on the mobile has changed all that. It broadens the universe of teenagers not only to sustain relationships that they have already made within their existing catchment area but also to dramatically extend this catchment by initiating relationships through chatlines and webclubs with people they have never met. There are dangers to this of course – at the time of writing, the UK was in trauma over the story of a 12-year-old girl who had eloped to Europe with a former US Marine she had 'met' over the Net. But, whatever the social dilemmas this raises over child or teenage personal safety, it has resulted in a generation of people who can 'bond' at a distance and who will continue to do so as adults – whether it is with friends, clients, suppliers or collaborators.

The commercial implications of this have been recognized for over a decade but the full impact has only just started to work its way through the market and the workplace as young consumers and workers with this level of Internet-comfort and savvy have begun to enter society as active adults.

The message was taken up by Eric Salama, group strategy director of the world's leading media group WPP, in a lecture on the new economy at the London Business School in September 2000.[4] Salama distinguishes in creative terms between those companies that are using technology to change fundamentally what they are offering their customers and those that are merely delivering electronically what they previously delivered through other methods. But he stresses that the key factor here is recognizing how fast and to what extent the expectations of the organization's customers are themselves being changed by their use of Internet and related technologies.

There is, he argues, drawing on theories outlined in the recently published *Blown to Bits*, a play-off between 'richness' – by which he means the establishment of a highly personalized relationship with the customer, usually involving human contact over the phone or face to face – and 'easy access' in any business transaction.

Much of the first wave of dot.com companies exploited the new technology by providing customers with easy access. Lastminute and Amazon both did this, playing on the fact that people didn't want to waste time setting up and attending a face-to-face meeting or even a phone call to make simple cost-based purchases they could just as easily make at the click of a mouse.

But there are still transactions where 'richness' is still an essential customer requirement and where transactions over the Net will not provide it. The creative twist is assessing just how much richness is required, in what form and how this is likely to change over what period of time. Salama explains:

Let's take financial services as an example. Ten years ago, most people would insist on seeing a representative from the company if they were buying a mortgage. Now, a growing number of people don't feel the need. They will use the Net to shop around to find the best supplier offering the most advantageous rate. But, nonetheless, most people will want a human being to speak to at the end of a phone before they make the deal and this is likely to remain the case for some time. This is why banks like First Direct, whose transactions are based on phone contact, are still rated more highly in terms of customer service than banks where transactions are conducted entirely online. The information I need could be provided through the computer but it is a comfort factor to speak to someone.

However if I am a well-heeled professional with a stock portfolio that needs managing, and trust and confidence in the individual is a key factor, this is a different matter entirely. I will want to get a feel for the manager's know-how, experience and integrity and this, at least for the moment, requires at least one and maybe regular meetings because the way I assess all this is likely to be as much through tacit signals as what he or she has to say.

Having said this, what we are finding at WPP is that it may be possible to provide even this level of richness using technological means in a few years' time. We have a stake in a company called Imagine, which is developing sophisticated voice-over and video-over IP technology that will enable me to conduct visual conversations with, say, my asset manager at the click of a button. Personally, I would still feel it important to meet the individual at least once but after that the technology would serve.

> But – who knows in an age when people get married over the Net – this too may change over time. The key for any businesses is assessing whether their customers' expectations in terms of richness and how it is delivered is ahead or behind the company's technology and what it can offer.[5]

Who knows indeed? In the three years since the lecture, the balance between access and richness is being redrawn by third-generation mobile phone technology. In addition to enabling users to take photographs and download material from the Internet, these phones will enable them to establish a video link with the people they are calling.

Project an Internet-savvy consumer group who are used to this kind of medium ten years forward in their lives, and the levels of customer 'intimacy' that are possible using already existing technology are almost limitless by today's standards. For example, the latest handsets already have colour screens and can download software remotely. Most attention has focused on the revolution this will trigger in mobile phone gaming, with a leading manufacturer, Informa, predicting that mobile-gaming revenues will reach $3.5 billion by the end of 2006.[6] However, linked to a company's intranet, the technology will also open up the possibility of remote video conferencing on the move, remote team working and, in the marketing field (see 'Branding Cool'), remote focus group discussions.

I will want to get a feel for the manager's know-how, experience and integrity and this, at least for the moment, requires at least one and maybe regular meetings because the way I assess this is likely to be as much through tacit signals as what he or she has to say.

Eric Salama, Group Strategy Director, WPP Group (worldwide media agency)

One of the most important gateways of the latest Web technology is that it opens up the possibility of dialogue with customers at every stage of the development of new products, services or propositions: from inception and early experimentation to trial testing and feedback.

This is particularly effective when the customer base is small, highly specialized but disparately located. Recognizing this fact has played a key role in helping GMT Games, a manufacturer of historical and military board games based in California, revolutionize the way they conduct their market research and product development.

Veteran game designer Gene Billingsley and graphic artist Rodger B. MacGowan founded GMT in 1990. Few people in the games industry would have given a company specializing solely in board games in this field good prospects. The older generation of history board gamers that had underpinned the industry in the previous three decades appeared to have lost interest and most of the new generation were attracted more to computer fantasy games such as Tomb Raider and WarHammer.

However, Billingsley calculated, shrewdly as it has turned out, that the veteran historical gamers had not lost interest in the hobby because they had 'grown out' of it. It was simply that they were bored with the games on offer that had become, in the late 1980s, over complex, poorly designed and targeted at 'anoraks': over-obsessive cliquey people who could spend hours on their hobby because they had precious little else to do in their lives.

Billingsley and MacGowan wanted to recapture the mainstream market with better designed games that were more fun and dynamic and could be played solitaire and between friends in the context of a routine social life, rather than solely in the clubs and conventions that had been the mainstay of the industry in the previous decade.

However, within five years of launching the company, they started to face problems. MacGowan had partnered with Billingsley in the first place because he had business sense as well as an interest in the hobby. Company after company in the industry had gone bust because the founders failed to appreciate that in a niche market, where products require painstaking design and high production values, accurately assessing the likely demand and time to market is the difference between life and death.

Games aimed at a mass market, such as Monopoly or Risk, very quickly turn into 'cash cows' because people go on buying them year in and year out. But historical gamers have specialist tastes. They like particular periods of history and their tastes are constantly in flux, not least because the last ten years has seen a renaissance in history and military writing and broadcasting, which has generated a demand for games covering previously uncharted periods. Keeping track of this demand is not easy. The cost of designing and producing games of this kind, and the cash flow implications, means one 'turkey' can kill a manufacturer almost overnight.

By the mid-1990s, the early success of the company meant that they had fuelled a demand for more games and were receiving a plethora of proposals from either in-house or independent designers for ones that covered everything from Greek mythology to the fighting in Bosnia. The extremely disparate nature of the marketplace, and the fact that less of the mainstream customers attended clubs and conventions (the traditional fora for market research), made it very hard for GMT to assess which games were likely to catch on fast and which would take so long to yield a return that it would endanger the company's financial future.

So, in 1997, Billingsley and MacGowan sat down with one of their associate designers, Tony Curtis, and came up with a new initiative, which they called Project 500. The idea was that details of games 'in embryo' would be posted to their regular subscribers and these would be invited to make credit card orders at a discount up front. This would provide the company with the finance it needed to produce the game. Billingsley calculated that 500 pre-orders would be sufficient to cover the costs of design and production and at the point when the company received the magic number, the game would go into production. In essence, they were reversing the conventional R&D relationship by letting the customers decide what games they were to produce rather than the designers.

To get customers to 'buy into' the idea, however, required that they see a level of detail that would be difficult to achieve using conventional mail-order materials. So the trio significantly upgraded the technology they were using on their website. Using the new-age JPEG files, the website can now provide highly detailed full-colour reproductions of the components of 'work in progress', such as rules, maps, counters and playing cards.

Originally intended solely to fuel P500 pre-sales, this technology has now taken the company into entirely new territory. Subscribers to the website are not only able to influence which games GMT produces but – by commenting on the components on view, when they are still being worked on by the designers – they are also able to become directly involved in the product's design.

Describing the dynamic this creates, Rodger MacGowan comments:

The clear, full-colour examples of maps, counters, cards and other components not only help stimulate P500 pre-sales. They allow customers to comment on whether they think the 'feel' and design on the game is right, which in turn enables the designer to adjust and improve on the work in progress.

The website also includes a regularly updated letter from the president, News From Gene, which creates a human contact with the company. Through these up-dates they get to know what we are thinking, what we are concerned about and, because the medium is interactive, how they can help us solve current problems.

In the old days, companies could only achieve this level of dialogue through 'game sessions' in particular towns where gamers were invited to play test games in progress in return for free sodas and snacks. Using the Internet, the same level of contact can be achieved to a far wider and more mainstream customer base.[7]

The innovations that have emerged have helped to make GMT the world's leading manufacturer of its type. As a result of feedback from subscribers to the website, for example, rules for some of the older games have been made simpler and more streamlined and the company has introduced a revolutionary new approach to historical gaming, where movement and events that affect counters on a map are triggered by the skilful playing of a hand of cards – rather like a game of poker or whist – rather than dice. This development alone, which could not have been refined without feedback from website subscribers, has placed GMT in an almost unassailable position in the industry.

Finally, the website has given GMT access to a new generation of young game players that they would previously have found almost impossible to target. 'An important piece of information we have gleaned from our interaction with fans on the website is that many of them are parents,' says McGowan, 'and that for many of them, playing our traditional games with their spouse and children was difficult because the games were perceived as too complicated and time-consuming.'

To this end, and as a direct result of the feedback they received over the website, MacGowan and Billingsley have launched a new division at GMT to design and produce historical games aimed at children aged ten and up that can be played by the whole family. A typical example is Ivanhoe: The Age of Chivalry, where players take on the role of a knight and use a series of cards and tokens to rally squires, gain the support of a maiden and win tournaments.

'We always wanted to tempt players back into the hobby who had played war games as teenagers and abandoned the hobby because they got married and couldn't carry it on because it didn't fit into their adult life,' MacGowan concludes. 'This latest development will, we hope, turn historical board gaming into a family activity and hopefully reach a new generation of gamers who might only have turned to computer games.'

LOYALTY

> *Grammar is disappearing – this is the first generation that is creating its own language with icons and mobile phones.*
>
> Martin Lindstrom, author of *Brandchild*

The willingness to initiate as well as sustain relationships at a distance also has a direct impact on the second key variable that influences Millennial behaviour: who or what they are loyal to.

We have already seen in 'The Provenance of Cool' that Millennials are most likely to be loyal, first and foremost, to friends in their own self-made community. This is not to say that, in the past, young people did not put their friendships first. Who forms part of this community, and how it develops over time, is what makes the difference today.

In previous generations, a hard core of friends established at school or college was built on significantly by people encountered in the workplace. Note the word *workplace*. These were, typically, people that boomers and Generation X literally 'bumped into' on a daily basis who, as friends encountered in the schoolyard and the college hall, shared the same work-based universe: in terms of place, clocking-off and clocking-on time, working environment, common issues (collective pay, collective gripes against the firm or a particular manager and so on) and, over time, experiences.

As the breakdown of 'job for life' security undermined the overarching loyalty between the individual and the organization in the 1980s and 1990s, the significance of workplace friendships as an emotional link to any one employer increased. A survey by international search consultants Sanders & Sidney in 2000[8] suggested that workplace friendship had become an important recruitment and retention aid. It concluded that the breakdown of traditional networks and the increase in divorce, single-person households and self-centred urban living meant that people were increasingly reliant on the workplace to provide their sense of belonging.

Employees in the survey claimed that emotional factors, such as friendship, were as important in binding them to an organization as traditional factors, such as pay and benefits. Over three-quarters of the respondents said that they made lasting relationships that extended beyond the workplace. For those facing redundancy, the loss of friend-ships and the resulting support network could be more sig-nificant than the loss of self-esteem or income.

But the conclusions of the Sanders & Sidney survey presuppose that a common workplace is the main incu-bator for friendships forged after school and college. This isn't necessarily the case for anything between a third and a half of the current workforces of developed economies who now work either from home or part-time and it is less likely to be the case for Millennials whose work life agen-das, as we will see below, are significantly different to those of boomers or Generation X.

When young professionals from these two previous generations first started to work from home, their attitudes were still rooted in a universe where 'full-time' work was the norm and a fixed workplace the centre of professional social culture. When Rank Xerox pioneered home-based working among its technical staff in the early 1980s, for in-stance, one of the attractions to the new breed of 'network-ers' was that they would still have access to the company's offices. This was not only seen by the networkers as a vital source of practical or technical support but also as a means of keeping them in touch socially.

The company's own surveys of their networkers' at-titudes to work illustrate vividly the extent to which a full-time office-based culture dominated in this period. Some networkers got dressed in a formal suit when they entered their own workrooms at home, even if they were not host-ing or visiting clients, because this 'validated' their view of themselves as 'real' workers.

Similarly, the design of the state-of-the-art corporate headquarters of British Airways in the late 1990s, based on the concept of an office-less meeting culture (see 'Crux'), still assumed that the 113-hectare site at Waterside, incorporating restaurants, bars, shops and a landscaped public parkland, would be the centre of commercial gravity – not only for staff permanently based there but also for the satellites of freelancers, consultants and independent workers that worked for them.

But as we saw in 'The Provenance of Cool', the new generation of Millennials are starting work with no preconception of a fixed corporate workplace as the norm. Their personal networks are typically not made up of people locked into mainstream culture and the incentives to get drawn into corporate workplaces as centres of their professional activity are therefore far less prominent.

The social infrastructures of Tom and Sophie and Owen and Sam, described in more detail in the previous chapter, illustrate this. In both his work running his own website-design firm and his increasing commitment to the rock group in which he plays bass guitar, Tom is motivated by the fact that his professional partners are former school or college mates who have purposefully eschewed a mainstream corporate career. His girlfriend Sophie, while working as a fashion assistant for a leading monthly periodical, draws her values and attitudes to work from her own membership of this circle rather than from her colleagues at work.

Similarly, Owen started his carpet-laying business to avoid the professional traps he perceived his parents fell into. While he acts as a subcontractor to a number of bigger construction firms, he has assumed none of their values or attitudes to work and would never consider joining them as permanent member of staff. His brother Al joined him as a partner after a deeply disillusioning period working full-time for an estate agent. His girlfriend Sam, while working in a full-time job, only does so because her immediate line manager is someone she respects. Her values are those of

Owen and his brother. She accepts full-time work on sufferance.

In both cases, these social infrastructures were created wholly outside mainstream corporate culture and, unlike the networks generated by Rank Xerox or British Airways, owe nothing to it other than a source of revenue. While the businesses run by Tom and Owen derive prestige from the fact that they have work from established clients, Tom and Owen as individuals derive no vicarious social status or self-esteem from the fact – among their own peers or in their own consciousness.

We have already outlined the implications to corporations as employers: where there is loyalty to the corporate ideal, it is likely to be local and based more on the leadership skills of the individual's own line manager than the company's corporate 'brand'. But there are also implications for their status as providers of goods and services.

Oceans of text and hot air have been devoted to how brand 'aware' the Millennial generation has been from an early age. The statistics are every bit as dramatic as those produced by adman and youth expert Merle Steir in the 1960s. A three-year-old child can recognize brand logos and brand loyalty can be influenced from the age of two. The average British, Australian or American child will be exposed to 20,000–40,000 ads a year. American children spend 60 per cent more time in front of the TV screen each year than they do at school.[9]

In the US, 4- to 12-year-olds spent about $35 billion in 2001 but influenced 60 per cent of their parents' brand purchases. Overall, their total global purchasing influence adds up to an unimaginable $188 trillion. According to Alison Quart,[10] branding by children extends into most areas of life. New York bar mitzvahs and birthday parties are becoming competitively extravagant status symbols. Teen movies have left behind the melancholic 'cinema of loneliness', epitomized by films such as *The Outsiders*, and embraced glossy makeover tales such as *She's All That*. Quart writes, 'Anyone can turn into a popular girl or prom queen, the films say. All it takes is a full commitment to beauty convention and the high school brand economy.'

She introduces us to high school students for whom even a university place is just another brand, albeit one of all-important status. The ambition of becoming a 'Harvard man' or a 'Williams girl' is so urgent that many parents will secure the services of a personal tutor, at up to $500 an hour. 'Packaging students,' explains one tutor, so sought after that she has become a brand of sorts in herself, 'is the name of the game.' In addition, students must also have great bodies, hence what Quart calls 'self-branding' – the stratospheric increase in teenage cosmetic surgery among girls, and use of special body-building supplements for teens by boys.

But for all this, being brand 'aware' does not mean automatically being brand 'loyal'. And where loyalty exists, while it may be intense, this does not mean that it is deeply rooted. It can vanish in an instant. It certainly cannot be inherited from previous generations.

> *Anyone can turn into a popular girl or prom queen, the [modern teen] films say. All it takes is a full commitment to beauty convention and the high school brand economy.*
>
> Alison Quart

Compare, for example, the contrasting fortunes of the brand image of two jeans companies over the past decade. No brand has done a better job in recent years than that of Tommy Hilfiger. When Hilfiger's distinctive logo-laden shirts and jackets started showing up on urban rappers in the early 90s, the company began sending researchers into music clubs to see how this influential group wore the styles. It bolstered its traditional mass-media ads with unusual promotions, from giving free clothing to stars on VH1 and MTV to a recent deal with Miramax Film Corp., in which teen film actors will appear in Hilfiger ads. Knowing its customers' passion for computer games, it sponsored a Nintendo competition and installed Nintendo terminals in its stores. Millennial-age consumers rewarded that attentiveness by making Hilfiger jeans their No. 1 brand in a recent American Express survey.

By contrast, Levi's, one of the world's most recognized brands and an icon of boomer youth, got a harsh wake-up call in 1997, when its market share slid and research revealed that the brand was losing popularity among teens. With its core boomer customers hitting middle age, both Levi's advertising and its decades-old five-pocket jeans were growing stale. 'We all got older, and as a consequence, we lost touch with teenagers,' says David Spangler, director of market research for the Levi's brand. Now, Levi's is fighting back with new ads, new styles, a revamped website and ongoing teen panels to keep tabs on emerging trends.

'We never put much muscle into this sort of thing before, but now, we are dead serious about it,' says Spangler. 'This is a generation that must be reckoned with. They are going to overtake the country.'[11] Marketers who don't bother to learn the interests and obsessions of Millennials, Spangler argues, are apt to run up against a brick wall of distrust and cynicism. Years of intense marketing efforts aimed directly their way have taught this group to assume the worst about companies trying to coax them into buying something. Ads meant to look youthful and fun may come off as opportunistic or simply naff.

In his book *Brandchild*, psychologist Martin Lindstrom argues that in keeping with the interactive computer culture into which they were born, Millennials grew up being radically more demanding of what they expected from creators of brand images.[12] The schoolyards in which they played may be 'brand showrooms' but Millennials wanted the opportunity to shape and tailor them to their own needs.

Brands, Lindstrom stresses, may have taken the place of religion in a godless world but paradoxically that makes individual brands more vulnerable, not less. Loyalties may be strongly felt but the need for instant gratification means that they can be dropped without a second thought. 'You're 100 per cent interactive – or dead,' he says. 'That's where you hit the wall. You can't build a brand on frustration.'

Furthermore, the tidal wave of brainwashing that children are subject to from cradle to college – the NeoPets.com website described above is a typical example – does not mean that by the time they become young adults they are brain-dead pawns in the hands of the corporate marketing department. The real revelation of the manipulative, unforgiving world of child marketing in the Internet age is, that having been on the receiving end of all this marketing-designed or sponsored focus group dialogue or interactive website probing since they were toddlers, most Millennials are more discerning and savvy about being sold to than their parents were.

As was vividly acknowledged in a widely read article in the UK journal *Marketing Week* in August 2002, the aura of effortlessness, authenticity and confidence that most commentators agree are the key constituents of being 'cool' cannot be bottled up and sprayed on brands that are produced by companies that patently do not espouse these values.[13]

Pointing to the abject and embarrassing failure of UK Prime Minister Tony Blair's attempt to brand his country as 'Cool Britannia' in the late 1990s as a warning light to big corporates rushing to fall into the same trap, the journal commented:

AWARENESS

It is doubtful whether a brand can ever be cool. Being 'cool' is not about 'increasing shareholder value' or 'enhancing lifetime value', the usual purpose of brands. The term may be vague but its origins are in youth counter-culture which has always been anti-establishment and views society in general (and brands in particular) as just another adjunct of capitalist power, ripe for subversion.

Consequently there is a contradiction, even an element of hypocrisy, among those brands that claim to be cool. They superficially adopt a rebellious stance towards power while actually trading on the very values their consumers despise.

In the electronic age, we all wear mankind as our skin.

Marshall McLuhan, University of Toronto

Millennials' hypocrisy barometers are more finely tuned than those of previous generations. Being aware means what it says: being AWARE. Precisely because they have been bombarded by more than 20,000 commercials a year, they know cant when they see it and have extremely low tolerance levels.

There is a lot more going on beneath the surface than fickle teens jumping on the latest trend. While some of Millennial-age teenagers' choices have been driven by faddishness and rebellion, marketing experts say those explanations are too simplistic.

'Most marketers perceive them as kids. When you do that, you fail to take in what they are telling you about the consumers they're becoming,' says J. Walker Smith, a man-

aging partner at Yankelovich Partners Inc., which special-
izes in generational marketing. 'This is not about teenage
marketing. It's about the coming of age of a generation.'[14]

Smith and others believe that behind the shift in Millennial icons and labels (see 'The Provenance of Cool') lies
a deep-seated shift in values. Having grown up in an even
more media-saturated, brand-conscious world than their
parents, they respond to ads differently, and they prefer to
encounter those ads in different places. The marketers that
capture Millennials' attention do so by bringing their messages to the places these kids congregate, whether it's the
Internet, a snowboarding tournament or cable TV. The ads
may be funny or disarmingly direct. What they don't do is
suggest that the advertiser knows Millennials better than
these savvy consumers know themselves. Soon, a lot of
other companies are going to have to learn the nuances of
Millennial marketing.

That's what happened to PepsiCo in its attempts to
earn Millennial loyalty with its Generation Next campaign,
says William Strauss, co-author of the 1991 book *Generations: The History of America's Future*. The TV ads, in which
kids showed off branded trinkets, from jackets to gym bags,
fell flat.[15]

'They were annoying', says Philip Powell, 14, of Hou-
ston, interviewed in Strauss's book. 'It was just one long
"Please, please, buy me".' Ironically, Pepsi already has one
of the biggest teen soda hits with Mountain Dew, but the
drink's success has little to do with advertising. Instead,
kids found out about Dew from their most trusted endorsers – each other.

'[Kids] believe – true or not – that they're the ones who
figured out and spread the word that the drink has tons of
caffeine,' explained top cool hunter Marian Salzman when
she was head of brand marketing at the leading US ad

agency Young & Rubicon. 'The caffeine thing was not in any of Mountain Dew's television ads. This drink is hot by word of mouth.'

Along with cynicism, Millennials are marked out by a distinctly practical world view, according to Salzman. Raised in dual-income and single-parent families, they've already been given considerable financial responsibility. Surveys show they are deeply involved in family purchases, be they groceries or a new car. One in nine high school students has a credit card co-signed by a parent, and many will take on extensive debt to finance college. Most expect to have careers and are already thinking about home ownership, according to a 1998 survey of college freshmen in North America.

And so we come full circle. As we saw earlier, a corporate employer's insight into the needs and aspirations are constrained by the fact that Millennials' self-made network of friends and similarly independent work peers cut them out of the loop from the very beginning of his or her contact with them. So, similarly, corporate marketers, and their agents, are wholly dependent on a combination of feedback and clues that they receive by observing from the outside the trends that emerge from these networks, rather like political Kremlin-watchers used to interpret the likely future attitudes of the Soviets.

Nor is the changing dynamics of Millennial-influenced loyalties and social awareness confined in its impact to the fields of HR management and brand marketing. The area most likely to be affected next is the increasingly important field of corporate social policy. The emerging fashionable doctrine of the decade is 'cause branding'. In the US, companies have put their names and resources to work supporting worthy causes deliberately to enhance their reputations, deepen employee loyalty, strengthen ties with business partners and even sell more products and services.

Leading the way has been the cosmetics giant Avon. In 1993 it committed itself to raising breast cancer awareness, particularly among medically underserved women, as an essential first step towards early detection of the disease. Avon's independent sales representatives now routinely distribute educational material on their sales calls and participate alongside customers in fund-raising walks. All told, Avon has raised and contributed nearly $300 million for the cause.

It is doubtful whether a brand can ever be cool.
Marketing Week, August 2002

ConAgra Foods, another pioneer of cause branding, has embraced the cause of combating child hunger by underwriting 100 after-school cafes now serving about one million hot meals each year. The programme, called Feeding Children Better, also encourages employees to raise money and serve meals, donates products and food trucks across the United States, and leads a national public-service advertising campaign to raise public awareness of child hunger.

In both cases, the companies have witnessed employees' rising commitment to the causes and, in the process, their own jobs, at a time when the wave of corporate wrongdoing that has emerged in the wake of the Enron and WorldCom scandals has left the US public clamouring for good corporate citizenship. Companies such as Avon and ConAgra Foods, which demonstrate a genuine sense of social responsibility, stand out in a world of increasingly undifferentiated goods and services.

According to a recent study on good corporate citizenship commissioned by Cone, a Boston-based consulting firm specializing in cause branding and marketing, 88 per cent of employees feel 'a strong sense of loyalty' to their employers. As many as 53 per cent of employees in the survey stated that they actually chose to work at the organizations partly because of their employers' expressed commitment to high-profile social issues.

Consumers, according to the survey, increasingly shop with a cause in mind and consider a company's support of social causes when deciding which products to buy and recommend to others. Aware of that trend, County Line, a ConAgra Foods brand, conducts an annual Christmas promotion in which it lets its customers know it will donate one per cent to its Feeding Children Better programme for every pound of County Cheese sold. In the past three years, the programme has raised more than $210,000.

However, as Cone's CEO Carol Cone acknowledges, company stakeholders – particularly the staff whose psychological sign-up to the cause is so important to the exercise, and especially those of Millennial age – are quick to sniff out where corporate do-gooding is being used as a cosmetic fig-leaf to distract attention from their less savoury activities elsewhere.

'Despite its many advantages, cause branding does have limitations and pitfalls. It is not, for example, an antidote for to a damaged reputation ... Nor can a cause ever turn a brand into something that it is not. A tobacco company, for example, might love to affiliate itself with an organization dedicated to fighting smoking by minors but the public wouldn't buy it, even if the organization's leadership did.'[16]

The simple fact is that Millennials are more savvy about serious social policy-making than their predecessors. 'Disaffected' youth were at the heart of British demos against nuclear weapons in the 1950s, against French corporatism in the 1960s, against American involvement in Vietnam in the 1960s and against Chinese political repression in the Tiananmen Square protests in 1989. But their disaffection was based on natural instincts of justice and equity rather than well-informed policy debates that they were directly a part of.

On the social policy issues of the first decade of the twenty-first century – corporate globalism and its impact on local markets and communities, transparent and account-able corporate and political governance, responsible environmental resource management – Millennial-age young people in developed countries are incredibly well informed. Ethics, environmental concern and political concepts and practice are part and parcel of the school and college curriculum. Students in primary, secondary and higher education will have taken part in role-play exercises, written essays and undertaken field research on the key issues.

As the organization and coordination of protests in Seattle, Bologna and Washington at meetings of the World Trade Organization or International Monetary Fund and at the annual assembly of key policy makers at Davos in Switzerland in recent years illustrate, the very technologies that promote Millennials in the workplace have also given them more prominence in the public arena. As *The Economist*'s survey of the young in 2000 pointed out: 'It is not that the young are necessarily angrier, it is just that, thanks to the Internet, they are able to communicate their anger better, organize themselves more effectively and recruit others to their cause more easily.'[17]

No (good) cause can ever turn a brand into something that it is not.

Carol Cone, founder, Cone (Boston-based cause branding consultancy)

But even the majority of Millennials who are not engaged in active protest can and do exercise their enhanced power as consumers and workers when they see organizations transgressing socially accepted ethical boundaries. Nike, leisurewear leader of the 1990s, found this out the hard way. Although still hugely popular among teens, the brand has lost its grip on the market in recent years, according to Teenage Research Unlimited, a Northbrook, Illinois, market researcher. Nike's slick national ad campaigns, with their emphasis on image and celebrity, helped build the brand among boomers, but they have backfired with Millennials.

'It doesn't matter to me that Michael Jordan has endorsed Nikes,' says Ben Dukes, 13, of LaGrange Park, Illinois, in the wake of Nike's disastrous attempt to sponsor Olympic snowboarders in 1999, after allegations of exploiting child labour in Malaysia and Indonesia sullied their name with him and millions of other Millennial-age teenagers.[18]

Nike and other manufacturers have found that success with this generation requires a new kind of advertising as well as a new kind of product. The huge image-building campaigns that led to boomer crazes in everything from designer vodka to sport-utility vehicles are less effective with them.

It is not that the young are necessarily angrier, it is just that, thanks to the Internet, they can communicate their anger better.

The Economist,
December 2000

'The old-style advertising that works very well with boomers, ads that push a slogan and an image and a feeling, the younger consumer is not going to go for,' says James R. Palczynski, retail analyst for Ladenburg Thalmann & Co. and author of *YouthQuake*, a study of youth consumer trends.

Instead, Millennials respond to humour (see 'The Provenance of Cool'), irony and unvarnished truth. Sprite has scored with ads that parody celebrity endorsers and carry the tagline 'Image is nothing. Obey your thirst'. J.C. Penney & Co.'s hugely successful Arizona Jeans brand has a new campaign showing teens mocking ads that attempt to speak their language. The tagline? 'Just show me the jeans.'

BALANCE

Stone Age Man worked only an estimated fifteen hours a week. In this new economy most of us will be working fifteen hours a day doing things that are far less risky than hunting for meat on the hoof, but sometimes equally stressful.

Peter Cochrane, head of research,
British Telecom

A fourth striking characteristic of Millennials is their unwillingness to be constrained by the same work–life constraints that have straitjacketed previous generations.

The work–life balance debate has been intimately wrapped up with a revolution in new work patterns that dates back 25 years. It first burst on to the scene in the early 1980s when employers, shaken by the job cuts they had been forced to make in the 1980/81 recession, hedged their bets and took on temps and people on short-term contracts in case the mid-decade recovery proved short-lived.

Almost all the work in the first half of the decade was created in this way. But, particularly in North America and the UK, where employment protection legislation had been reined back, much of it was low paid, low status and insecure. Trade unions refused to represent what they saw as casual labour because they feared its increase might further undermine the status of their full-time members.

Few temps or casuals were protected by the law and the terms used by lawyers and civil servants to describe them – 'marginals', 'atypical workers', 'peripheral staff' – confirmed the fact that in almost everybody's eyes, staff working full-time on a permanent basis was still not only the norm but also the social ideal.

What changed all this was the dawning realization that the fastest growing section of the workforce – women – might not actually aspire to this ideal. Aided by a dramatic but short-lived drop in the number of school leavers entering the market at the end of the decade – which made retaining or re-recruiting older workers a priority – employers started offering women well-paid, high-status part-time work. Unions, devastated by savage drops in their 'full-time' members, also started seeing these workers as a lucrative source of new blood.

The result was a 'family friendly' employment revolution. Career-break schemes, job sharing, professional part-time working and home-based working boosted the number of so-called 'atypical workers' to a massive 50 per cent of the workforce on both sides of the Atlantic by the mid-1990s. But the rationale for these schemes remained the assumption that the main reason why both women and men would want to work in this way was because they were parents.

By the turn of the millennium, the agenda had changed yet again. Any attempt to regulate employment patterns by law had been effectively thrown out of the window by governments of whatever political hue. A combination of global commercial expansion unleashed by the collapse of Communism and the Internet revolution meant that big international corporations had the desire and the means to encourage their key professionals to work at any time and in any location.

'Family friendly' political agendas were replaced by 'work–life balance' agendas, in an attempt to combat the emerging long-hours culture. Now the thrust of both government-funded employment schemes and regulatory frameworks was to combat the stress of working in the office (and at home) at all hours rather than (or as well as) the stress caused by an inability to reconcile professional and parental responsibilities.

This is where we are today. But the rationale behind where we are is still way behind the times. Just as family friendly employment policies presupposed that in most people's lives there was 'work' and 'family', and nothing else, so work–life balance schemes presuppose that there is 'work' and 'life', and that the two are wholly separate.

The reality of course is that in an age where you can 'work' anywhere and at any time, you can also 'live' anywhere and at any time – and that the artificial distinction between the two is increasingly meaningless. Millennials are at the cutting edge of the debate. Michael Willmott[19] argues that while the bulk of the demand for 24-hour living resides with 30- to 50-year-olds who are convenience driven – who are looking for solutions to their time problems under the pressure of an intense professional lifestyle – their willingness to extend routine daytime tasks into 'unsocial' hours is born of necessity, not proactive choice.

The enthusiastic race into the new frontier of nighttime living is being led by 'fast-laners', who amount to a quarter of the population. These, by Willmott's definition, are the people who really enjoy the 24/7 culture. 'They tend to be under 30 and without children. They feel fairly time-pressured but do not think that the pace of life is too fast and they believe that their lives would be enhanced if services were available 24 hours a day.' Their view of the 24-hour society, he concludes, is hedonistic and bound up with the immediate satisfaction of their wants. Everybody else feels forced into living 24/7 lives. They desire it (see below).

TIME USERS: FOUR TYPES

1 *Fast-laners* (25 per cent of adults): these are the people who enjoy the 24-hour culture. They tend to be under 30 and without children. They feel fairly time-pressured but do not think that the pace of life is too fast and they believe that their lives would be enhanced if services were available 24 hours a day. Their view of the 24-hour society is hedonistic and bound up with the immediate satisfaction of their wants.

2 *Convenience driven* (28 per cent of adults): this is the family group, aged between 30 and 50, often of two working parents with dependent children. This group is the most time-pressured (over 90 per cent), who also complain that the pace of life is too fast. They are very much in favour of 24-hour service, which they see as a pragmatic solution of their time problems.

3 *Pressured conservatives* (19 per cent of adults): this is a middle-aged group with older children. They feel some time pressures and that the pace of life is too fast (but at lower levels than the convenience driven). They do not support 24-hour service and think it unnecessary, taking a somewhat moralistic view about its desirability.

4 *Past-timers* (27 per cent of adults): this is an older age group, most of whom are 60 years or above and whose children have left home. The large majority are retired and as a group they do not themselves feel time pressured but believe the world is now moving too fast. They see no need for 24-hour service; rather, they would like the world to slow down and be like it was in the past.

Source: The Future Foundation

This dynamic – the 24/7 young lead the way, the time-pressured professionals follow – is very evident in the current moves by the Greater London Authority (GLA) to transform Britain's capital into a 24-hour city.

London's ambition's to become a 24-hour city are not unique or even novel. They follow a decade in which a variety of cities in North America and Europe have transformed their own culture and economies by extending the time in which the streets 'live'.

The US model, most effectively achieved in Seattle and San Francisco, is based on the concept of reviving the 'downtown' or central business district of the town, and the immediate neighbouring areas. Instead of a wholesale exodus from these commercial areas at the end of the 'working' day, people are encouraged to stay or return through a variety of measures that form part of an urban planning strategy. These include building attractive residential neighbourhoods in and around business districts, reliable and late-serving public transport to move people in and out and day and night entertainment, shopping and pedestrian facilities.

The European model, closely inspired by the US lead, is to create what the Italians call *la passeggiata*: a sense of the individual mingling with other people and being part of the space, of streets filled with people day and night, walking, sitting, watching and being watched. This has been a central feature of Copenhagen for more than two decades and was extended to Barcelona in the wake of the 1992 Olympics by creating 150 new public squares.

It also inspired the (architecturally) revolutionary design of the new British Airways headquarters, Waterside, designed by Swedish town planner Niels Torp. This was designed to promote an office-free culture in which meetings took place in a corporate boulevard that linked all the business units, with its own shops, cafes and restaurants. *La passeggiata* was uppermost in Torp's thoughts when he came up with the design. The idea was that 'creativity' would be inspired by 'serendipity' as people discussed their business not in stuffy Anglo-Saxon meeting rooms but in a common space designed to reproduce the dynamo of a thriving European cafe society. This was supposed to extend into the small hours. Waterside was intended by its designers to be a 24-hour facility, though British management conservatism and the recession in the airline industry brought about by September 11 has so far put paid to these aspirations.

The US and European models of the 24-hour city was designed for and embraced by a broad section of the population. In the UK, Millennials have been the movers and shakers of the whole movement. The pioneer city, Manchester, is home to over 100,000 students – the largest concentration of students in Europe – and is one of the gay capitals of the world. It has a thundering evening economy of bars, restaurants and entertainment and its regeneration from an industrial giant of the past to a thoroughly post-modern city of the twenty-first century was founded on exploiting this resource.

Their [fast-laners] view of the 24-hour society is hedonistic and bound up with the immediate satisfaction of their wants.

Michael Willmott, the Future Foundation (future trends research agency)

The city's ability to increase the residential population of its central district tenfold during the 1990s was based on its relaxed approach to licensing and planning, allowing an eclectic approach to development that is part and parcel of 24/7 urban living.

This is also London's start-point. The strategy is predicated on the astonishing growth of a late-night entertainment industry almost entirely created by Millennials. The

GLA estimates suggest that half a million young people regularly go clubbing on a Saturday night – more than all the people who visit all of London's 'top ten' visitor attractions combined in a week.[20] As such, the GLA argues, it is an integral part of the capital's growing entertainment and tourism sector which now employs over 300,000 people (eight per cent of the total UK workforce), boosting London's image as a World City that is at the leading edge of 'excitement and creativity'.

In turn, this industry means better transport, cleaning and (given the central role of drink and possibly drugs in all-night clubbing) policing. This in itself will boost opportunities for employment and 'overtime' in the relevant industries but the chain-reaction goes much further:

- Public transport services (bus, tube, tram) are extended to 3–4 a.m. to transport home the half million people on a Friday and Saturday night who surge into London's West End between 10.30 and midnight in order to club.
- This opens up new opportunities for entertainment, drinking and catering businesses other than clubs – pubs, restaurants, take-away joints, cafes, bars – to extend their hours, aided by more liberal licensing regulations.
- This in turn opens up new job opportunities for those people willing and able to work 'unsocial' hours, particularly among the local population where there are often high levels of unemployment – not only in the later-night entertainment industries but also in public transport, security, street cleaning and public information services.
- As transport and essential local service infrastructures expand to meet this new late-night demand, so it becomes easier for other businesses located in the district, for example genuinely global corporations operating on

a 24-hour basis and all-night supermarkets, to run skeleton night-time operations safely and efficiently.

- This in turn generates a demand for late-night services currently operating on a Friday and Saturday night to be extended to other days. Thus, a wide range of businesses – shops, job agencies, Internet cafes, cinemas, sandwich bars, museums and tourist attractions etc. – get in on the act.
- Initially the workforce to staff these businesses is drawn from 'fast-laners' and the local unemployed but then, as the whole concept of late-night working is mainstreamed, convenience-driven adults with families start extending their own working hours. The whole process is aided by the fact that offices or shops run by a skeleton site-based staff can increasingly be supported by a far larger home-based workforce connected to the business by computer.

In this sense, the move to a 24/7 society conforms closely to the analogy American sociologist Murray Melbin created when he compared night to the frontier in the Old West. In his seminal book *Night as Frontier*,[21] he saw a direct contrast between the shortage of land then and the shortage of time now. 'A frontier,' according to Melbin, 'is a new source of supply for sustenance or profit. It is a safety valve for people who feel confined.' And, like in the Old West, unmarried young people with few ties (and wild behaviour) led the way followed by settlers who normalized the move into uncharted territory.

Already the night-time frontier is moving ever outwards. The Centre for Advanced Spatial Analysis at London's University College charted the main centres of London's evening economy. Apart from discovering that there are more people on the West End's pavements between 10.30 p.m. and midnight than at any other time of the day, they found comparable concentrations at the same time in fashionable or busy inner and outer suburbs as far removed as Earls Court, Islington, Chelsea, Kingston, Hampstead, Rayners Lane and Shoreditch.[22] At the time of writing, proposals to provide 24-hour licences to selected venues in designated 'Entertainment Management Zones' was being lobbied for by the Greater London Authority.[23]

> *A frontier [in time or space] is a new source of supply for sustenance or profit. It is a safety valve for people who feel confined.*
>
> Murray Melbin, author,
> *Night as Frontier*

24-CITIES: STRATEGY START-POINTS

- San Francisco and Seattle: *downtown regeneration*: attract 24-hour living into previously commercial districts by building residential housing in neighbouring districts and tempting workers back into the district through late-night or all-night entertainment/culture.
- Copenhagen and Barcelona: *city-wide regeneration through* la passeggiata: building a city of squares. Cafes and streets filled with people walking, sitting, watching and being watched – in both leisure and work settings – at whatever hour.
- Manchester and London: *Millennials-driven*: take advantage of inner-city club culture to attract more people into the city centre late at night through better transport and urban services offered either on a late-night or all-night basis.

LONDON'S LATE-NIGHT ECONOMY

- 500,000 young people go 'clubbing' in London on a Saturday night – more than all the people who visit all of London's 'top ten' visitor attractions combined in a week.
- More people leave Leicester Square on a Saturday night at 11 p.m. than at any other time of the day.
- More people walk the streets of the West End between 10.30 p.m. and midnight than at any other time of the day.

Source: Centre for Advanced Special Analysis, London University College

---

RISK

The young do not know enough to be prudent and therefore they attempt the impossible – and achieve it generation after generation.

Pearl S. Buck

A final defining characteristic of Millennials is their attitude to risk. Two very different and slightly contradictory observations have been made about the risk-friendly nature of under-25 decision-making. The first is that Millennials are baggage free, born into an era of more frenetic change than their parents and thus making them better adapted for the frenetic world they are about to enter.

The second is that, as Pearl S. Buck commented half a century ago, Millennials are risk free because they don't know any better. This generation may have been born into

an era where there is no longer a job for life but their formative years have been spent, at least in the developed world,
in an era of unparalleled prosperity.

The best way to examine this is to look at the shifting
way in which the attitudes and behaviour of Millennials has
been covered in the USA, as the world's biggest economy
moved from an unprecedented period of prosperity in the
1990s to plateau in the early years of the following decade.

At the turn of the millennium, at the height of the
dot.com stock market bubble, the point repeatedly made
of Millennials is that they were spoilt by their parents and
'had it' better than any of their predecessors. The Millennial
generation was the most well-educated group in the United
States in the last century, according to the US Department
of Education's 2000 statistics. They were also among the
most privileged, 'coming of age at a time of continuing
prosperity'.

The vast majority of them expected both parents to
work. According to Denver-based Claire Raines, co-author
of *Generation at Work*, Millennials' baby-boomer parents
see themselves as devoted, and will do whatever it takes to
be good parents: weekly soccer matches, dance and karate
classes, computer camps and so on.

Indeed, according to the Roper Youth Report, published by New York city-based Roper Starch Worldwide, 82 per cent of kids aged 8 to 17 felt that they
are very or somewhat likely to have a better life than
their parents; 37 per cent of 17-year-olds said they
are very likely to have a better life than their parents.
'This is a reflection that many of these kids, like their parents, are receiving an almost constant avalanche of good
economic news,' commented Peter Silsbee, vice-president
at Roper Starch. 'And one of the tributaries of that river to
the waterfall of economic news is news about young peo-

ple – 20-year-olds – who are benefiting from the Internet economy. Kids experience a gold rush mentality regarding the Internet.'

Surveys in *Business Week* and *The Economist* were full of statistics like the Bureau of Labour's in the United States in 2000 that nearly a fifth of high school students own shares and many actively trade them – and the fact that, in a reversal of its longstanding rules, Harvard University had struck down a ban on student businesses run from dormitories, because prospective alumni were threatening to go elsewhere unless they could bring their high school companies with them.[24]

The next two years took a lot of the gloss away from this shiny perception of the world. The dot.com crash in the spring of 2001 removed the no-risk idealism away from brash new start-ups. In addition, unlike before, the latest downturn has hit teenagers and young adults disproportionately, compared with older workers. In the United States, at the time of writing, the current unemployment rate was hovering around 5.8 per cent, a six-year high. The proportion of jobless teenagers aged 16 to 19 had climbed to 16 per cent. Among workers aged 20 to 24, the figure was about 9.6 per cent.[25]

Suddenly, Millennials turned back into a generation that had something to learn from their parents. Because if boomers and Generation X have a lot to learn from their children about technology, they do know all there is to know about economic downturns.

So, according to Bruce Tulgan, author of *Winning the Talent Wars* and *Managing Generation Y*, in an article in a leading US personnel journal in March 2002, workers under 25 should take a lesson from their older relatives in Generation X.[26] Tulgan commented:

> *Generation Xers started their careers in the late 1980s and early 1990s, amidst the first waves of downsizing and restructuring. They adopted a free-agent mindset as a response to the death of job security. Gen-Yers picked up the free-agent mindset, but theirs was driven by a boom mentality.*
>
> *This recession may be a blessing for them. While Gen-Y workers tend to be technically savvy, voracious learners, highly confident, and ambitious, they have lacked the feeling of vulnerability, and an understanding of the uncertainty that characterizes the real new economy.*

The US experience on this issue is important to note because almost all the generational theories about Millennials – as indeed those of baby boomers and Generation X – developed out of North American marketing-led consumer studies. The notion of Generation Y as free agents is also, in part, a by-product of the fact that Americans link 'freedom' with entrepreneurial go-getting – a subset of the American dream.

In other countries, the social uncertainties shaping Millennial-age attitudes and behaviour may be the same, but the ideal end point is not so clear-cut. For example, in Japan disillusionment with the post-war social contract is as great with the Millennial generation as it is in other developed economies but the result has been apathy rather than empowerment.

Young people in Japan often feel alienated from their *sarariman* (salarymen) fathers, who worked too hard at their jobs to establish much of a relationship with their children. Japanese firms have stopped hiring and youth unemployment is high. Families are prepared to support adult children almost indefinitely. But in the absence of any alternative aspiration to the old corporate job for life ethic, such as the role model of the dot.com young entrepreneur that exists in the UK and US, this has left teenagers and young adults purposeless. A new sub-class of what commentators in the country call *hikikomori* (literally people who withdraw) has emerged, many of whom, according to local social surveys, are young men obsessed with role-playing videogames, comics and television, and young girls rebelling against conformity by being sexually promiscuous.

'My view is that young people have given up,' said Motohiro Moroshima, a leading business professor at Japan's Keio University in 2000. 'They've lost hope of making a change. They were also too spoiled to be entrepreneurial and to make the changes themselves.'

In an interview for *The Economist* in 2000, Moroshima painted a picture of a generation of lost souls, with millions choosing to become 'freeters', doing a series of casual and part-time jobs while they figure out what to do with their lives.[26] 'The one thing they're sure of is that they do not want to be like their fathers,' he concluded. 'And the girls don't want to be with boys who are like their fathers, so the boys are sure not be.'

The combination of affluence and conformity has wrought similar social problems among Millennials in Germany. As in Japan, most of today's German teenagers and young adults have never known poverty and, unlike their parents, they are not motivated by nation building. A conservative financial industry has not translated technological opportunities into an entrepreneurial revolution, as it has in the United States and in Britain. Most of the Internet companies that have been established, such as Internetshop and Ricardo.de, were in fact started by former management consultants in their 30s and 40s.

'Risk', in Millennials as well as their parents and elder siblings, is bound up closely with local cultural influences and role models as well as social history and family mores. Nearly all countries with highly developed economies have seen job-for-life and pension security erode or disappear during the past decade. In some this has resulted in a generation better adapted to an era of rapid change than their parents, who can and will walk away from employers who fail to engage their talents effectively or who rat out on their promises. In others, rebellion against the status quo has taken very different outlets.

> *Recession may be a blessing for them (Millennials). While Generation Y workers tend to be technically savvy learners, highly confident and ambitious, they have lacked the feeling of vulnerability, and an understanding of the uncertainty that characterizes the real new economy.*
>
> Bruce Tulgan, author of *Managing Generation Y*

SUMMARY

Cool hunting is neither new nor universally applicable. It dates back to the first attempts to explain and target youth counterculture in the 1960s. Then, as now, it was consumer and advertising led. Terms like 'yuppie', 'wigger', 'metrosexual' and 'freeter' have influenced how social trends in the past four decades have been popularly seen and interpreted – but they focus primarily on how people behave as consumers.

We have tried in this chapter to explain the long-term implications of Millennial attitudes and behaviour through a number of key words:

- *Intimacy*: In contrast to the two previous generations, Millennials grew up with Internet and mobile phone technology as a primary means of communicating with their friends and peers. Again in contrast to boomers and Generation X, they commonly use these technologies to initiate relationships as well as (as is more usually the case with older people) sustaining relationships that have already been forged face to face. This has the potential to transform the way in which work-based networks and customer relations are conducted in the future. Firms that are fully part of the 'new economy' will be distinguished by their ability to exploit this.

- *Loyalty*: Millennials' primary loyalty is to an immediate social circle that it is entirely of their own creation and, far more than was the case in previous generations, owes little or nothing to mainstream corporate culture. This means that, both in terms of recruitment or retention and brand marketing or product development, corporations are working strictly from the outside and are heavily reliant on focus group feedback and attitude-based field research to inform campaigns directly targeted at teenagers and young adults.

- *Awareness*: Precisely because they have been on the receiving end of up to 20,000 commercial messages a year, Millennials are far more aware of circumstances when they are being deliberately manipulated and have a far lower tolerance of cant and hypocrisy. Traditional brand awareness strategies simply do not work. Millennials are far more likely to respond to campaigns (recruitment or brand marketing) based on irony, humour (see 'The Provenance of Cool') and unvarnished truth than sophisticated image-building. The growing field of cause branding, where a company's image and staff relations are transformed by a focused support for needy social causes, will only work if there is a clear link between the firm's values and culture and its professed social ideals.

- *Balance*: Millennials have been at the cutting edge of 24/7 living. Unlike previous generations, which have extended family and professional responsibilities into 'unsocial' hours reluctantly under time pressures, un-attached young adults (fast-laners) have actively em-braced the 24-hour culture. Their view is hedonistic and bound up with the immediate satisfaction of their wants. As a result, they have fuelled the development of new evening and night-time economies, particularly in the UK, which over time will open up employment and commercial opportunities to a broader cross-section of society.

- *Risk*: Perceptions of Millennials as baggage-less free agents have been subject to some change in recent years. This view was US-led and heavily influenced by the American-generated economic boom of the 1990s and the turn of the century dot.com bubble. When this bubble burst in 2001 and the economy plateaued, this heady optimism collapsed. Millennials are undoubtedly free of the cultural attachment boomers and Generation X had to the post-World War II promises of a job for life and pension-based security. But their aspirations and capabilities as entrepreneurial free thinkers are largely determined by local cultural influences, social circum-stances and family mores.

INSIDE COOL

4

Mozart: Don't worry. I've finished the Requiem.
Salieri: You have? Can I see it?
Mozart: Not yet. It's still in my head.

Peter Shaeffer, Amadeus

When it comes to responding to the employment challenges raised by the last chapter, our money is on Ricardo Semler, president of the Brazilian engineering conglomerate Semco. This is not because he always comes up with the right answers – as we will see in 'Cool Leadership', Semler's quick-fire prescriptions may not be applicable to everyone – but because he asks the right questions.

Before he took over his father's corporation, one of Brazil's biggest, he wanted to be a rock musician and helped to found and run a college group. Like all garage-created rock outfits, nobody had to be there if they didn't actively choose to be. So, just as the drummer in his band could not be persuaded to turn up at rehearsal if he didn't feel motivated, he reasoned that staff at Semco would only really contribute to the company on a grey Monday morning if the atmosphere in which they work kept them feeling excited.

'When employees are given control [over the way they work] they act in their own interest, which will be in the interest of the business,' he commented in a recent interview.[1] 'We believe in the virtues of dissent. We don't want a crowd of workers singing the company song. We listen, and if the dissenter is right, maybe we can all learn something.'

FINDING A NEW 'WHY'

There is nothing worse about old age than having nothing to show for it but a long life.

Seneca, Roman senator and philosopher

We agree. The first big question any employer has to ask in an age influenced by the Millennial attitudes explored in the last chapter is: Why are our staff coming into work?

This is not the start-point for another quality crusade lecture about keeping people motivated by providing them with commercial vision. It always was a false premise because the thing that was supposed to keep people turned on in the total quality era – the success of the company and its own board-created values – was actually a total turn-off to most of the staff. Regardless of whether people signed up to the company mission, they were going to turn up anyway.

But, as we have seen in the last chapter, this is not the case now. Millennials, and an increasing number of their baby-boomer and Generation X predecessors, are free from all the baggage that keeps them in work out of duty or social orthodoxy. As Bruce Tulgan, author of *Managing Generation X* commented: 'Dues-paying is an obsolete concept for Xers who face an employment market that offers no hope of long-term job security with any one employer.'[2]

If that was true when he wrote the book ten years ago, it is a sure-fire certainty now.

Moreover, the tantalizing challenge facing employers in a knowledge economy is that the asset they most want to tap with their key professional staff – what is going on in their heads – is the asset they are least able to control.

Chloe Alexander, a personal development coach who has worked extensively with young professionals who have entered employment in the last decade, puts it this way: 'In relationship terms, young professionals and their employers are seriously on the rocks. Companies want to be loved without loving back: they expect the devotion of staff without rewarding them in kind. In prestige industries, such as media and finance, organizations are increasingly reluctant to grant long-term job security. Employees are expected to accept uncertainty as a way of life.'[3]

In response to this, she stresses, young professionals are becoming less complacent and are revising their goals. 'When people see that employers won't commit to them, they reciprocate in kind. The 20–30 age group is self-reflective and self-critical. They know that they can't hang on to the company's apron strings, and are starting to ask themselves fundamental questions about what they really want to do, and what they are really about.'

Dues-paying is an obsolete concept for Yers who face an employment market that offers no hope of long-term job security with any one employer.

Bruce Tulgan,
Managing Generation Y

Not that this self-reflection has anything 'soft' about it. Millennials are the most individualistic generation to hit the labour market. They think differently, are more entrepreneurial and are vastly more independent. And individuals are, well, individual. They respond to change in different ways and have agendas that do not always neatly tie in with those of their employers. Moreover, if an individual, whether they are an assembly line worker or an R&D boffin, has an idea that might transform the company's fortunes, then they are sitting on a negotiable asset.

Putting it at its bluntest, they have it and the organization hasn't. They might need the organization's resources to make it reality but they can just as easily turn to another firm or even raise the necessary resources themselves, with a bigger payback for themselves.

This turns the conventional relationship between the individual and the organization on its head. If organizations want to tap the innovative potential of their staff, then they have to provide an environment and a set of motivations that will foster and support this potential.

It is also worth stressing that in the absence of the organization being able to guarantee long-term job security – a guarantee that this generation, as we have already seen, may not want or need anyway – the only thing that counts, both as a determining factor of the relationship and a negotiable asset, is what is going on in the employee's head.

The best way of illustrating this is by confronting one of the paradoxes of modern business strategy – why mergers and acquisitions designed to forge a synergy of the two players' strengths wind up saddling the newly created organization with an inheritance of their weaknesses rather than their strengths.

The rot starts from the very beginning. Maintaining 'business as usual' reassurances as the basis of an early communications campaign, the natural instincts of many boards, is nearly always seen by the staff they most want to keep as an insult to their intelligence. The first rumour of merger talk will have already caused their mental state to jump from green to red alert.

The best and therefore the most sought after people see the process not as a threat but as an opportunity to further their careers. The most valuable card they can put on the table is also the least quantifiable: their creativity, and through it the added value they bring to their job. If the organization fails to respond sufficiently early or proactively, the best individuals will draw their own conclusions and start looking for alternatives, if not in deadly earnest at least as a way of hedging their bets. If they start looking, it's an odds-on bet (except in the very deepest of recessions) that they will find – and, as we have seen earlier, their departure may not occur immediately but after six months or a year when their contribution is most needed.

As UCLA's Karen Stephenson, the world's leading expert of professional networking, concludes: 'The early stages of any change management process are like a Turkish bazaar, where the best people want to know "what's in it for them" so that they can make the right career decision. Officially, these issues are dealt with in public only after the formalities are over, but the real barter process needs to take place earlier and in private. If you keep your most creative people in the dark, they aren't likely to stay around to see what's on offer and if they do, they will keep their best ideas back.'[4]

In relationship terms, young professionals and their employers are seriously on the rocks. Companies want to be loved without loving back: they expect the devotion of staff without rewarding them in kind.

Chloe Alexander, personal development coach

Nor does it stop there. This form of 'psychological work-to-rule' will continue until they remain reassured months or even years down the line. Their best ideas, their best insights, their best personally held market intelligence will remain – just as Mozart's *Requiem* did for Salieri – in their heads. Forget any appeal to loyalty. Forget any residual sense of team spirit. Forget stock or pension funds that will accrue ten or twenty years down the line. What counts is the perception that the newly merged company will be cutting new ground and that there will be plenty of reflected glory and insight. As a senior editor of US journal *Fortune*, Kenneth Labiche wrote recently: 'Your workers haven't been evincing much energy and talent lately? Maybe that's because they don't trust the company to reward these qualities and perhaps that's because the company doesn't trust the workers to exhibit them.'[5]

No example illustrates this more than the comedown of the Time Warner–AOL merger, an alliance between old media and new media that, to quote *The Economist* in January 2000, 'has the potential to change the competitive landscape so fundamentally that nothing can be the same again.'[6]

Three years after all the hyperbole, with the new group worth only a quarter of its peak valuation of $260 billion, Time Warner marked the anniversary by shedding Steve Case, the founder of AOL and the architect of the deal. However, Case was not the problem. The underlying cause of the rot was the clash of cultures, most importantly in how to successfully manage the tension between creative freedom and operational control. The attraction of getting into bed with Time Warner for AOL was that it opened up access to highly attractive new content, brought vast new investment for new projects and, like all big companies, the ability to squeeze more profit out its operations than a small company.

The early stages of any change management process are like a Turkish bazaar, where the best people want to know 'what's in it for them' so that they can make the right career decision … if you keep your most creative people in the dark, they aren't likely to stay around to see what's on offer and if they do, they will keep their best ideas back.

Professor Karen Stephenson, UCLA

The disadvantage is that it brought corporate politics and in-fighting that alienated AOL's tightly knit team spirit and undermined the light hand Case had on the tiller. The theory behind Case's appointment as chairman of the new group was that it gave an old media company a new-generation boss who was young (41) and totally in touch with the possibilities of the Internet. The reality was that Case was in charge of a sprawling corporation with six times the number of employees, and poisonous in-fighting between its divisions.

Caught up in this, AOL's best people walked or drew in their creative claws. None of the architects of the original deal remain in charge. Few of their deputies remain and those that do are completely demoralized. Far from the merger ushering in a new dawn of Internet-led initiatives, it is a succession of old media assets such as *Lord of the Rings* and the *Harry Potter* films that keeps the industry afloat.

'What the hell were we thinking when we thought that mergers, gadgets and convergence theories were in themselves going to be any other than a distraction,' Peter Chernin, Rupert Murdoch's right-hand man at News Corp., said in the wake of Case's departure. 'Where did [the industry] get our grandiose ideas that the media business was on the way to complete an utter reinvention because a few people at the top of the organization signed a deal that no one else had ownership of.'[7] His point was that what made AOL strong was the common ownership that a small well-knit company was able to foster in its staff and that learning or re-learning how to achieve this was the only thing that was going to revitalize the business.

If he wants an example, he need look no further than HBO, the one shining star in the Time Warner AOL firmament and the creator of such hit series as *Sex in the City* and *Band of Brothers*. HBO's secret has been twofold: the creation of a small boutique-style identity within a huge corporate institution and the granting of creative independence within a tightly controlled operation.

Employing just under 2000 people, less than two per cent of the group, HBO is physically and operationally removed from the group's other activities, notably Warner

Brothers in Los Angeles. The current boss, Chris Brewster, has been there 17 years and has made a deliberate attempt to liberate creative people in order to keep pushing at the edges of television drama. 'We all know what we are looking for,' said one HBO executive. 'We know how to smell it.' Nobody even suggests merging New York-based HBO with other Time Warner studios. The company has learned its lesson.

Managing Millennials, then, is about mental engagement. Recent research by Caroline Buller from the Cranfield School of Management on what young MBA alumni want from their school confirms this. Most of the 1200 alumni she interviewed are less interested in short-term 'fill a hole' training designed to meet the need of their current job and paid for by their employer, who they see as the main beneficiary – and more interested in events that reproduce the atmosphere of cutting edge that they experienced studying for an MBA. Many feel that conventional executive education fails to capture this dynamic and is too focused on specialist interests to meet their broader learning needs.

'What alumni are saying to us,' says Buller, 'is "tell me something that I didn't know I needed to know. Challenge me. Astonish me." If the session is led by a well-known professor, they do not want well-polished presentations based on his well-polished theories. They want him to explore dangerous territory and ideas on the cutting edge, where they can make their own contribution to emerging concepts and be present while they emerge.'[8]

Challenge. Astonish. Tell staff something they didn't know they needed to know. Keep them mentally engaged so their broader life agenda loses out by not staying. Make the time they spend with you the important part of their 24/7 lives. It's a different agenda from the days when a salary rise and a non-contributory pension fund did the trick. But the ride could be interesting. As *Fast Company*, the bible of new business philosophy, put it: 'If you want your company to think outside a box, why not learn by working with people who don't know there is a box?'[9]

But what does this actually mean in practice?

TURNING THE SWITCH ON

> *Ideas are what count. You can find competent sub-ordinates to do everything else.*
> Michael Eisner, chairman and chief executive, the Disney Corporation

Millennials may think faster and make decisions quicker, but the way these decisions and ideas are informed or inspired is little different from anyone else. Our work on how ideas are inspired and shaped inside organizations – conducted for the UK management centre the Roffey Park Institute (see 'Brainstorming Cool') – suggests that the best breakthroughs in thinking are triggered outside a work setting and draw on formative influences that extend way beyond the latest Peter Drucker book.

For example, we saw how myth and fantasy help to shape the minds of Millennials, creating a set of mental and visual references that can be drawn on in their adult life. A recent survey of 368 US college students, for example, found that mental images created in movies and television were rated by the students as a far more valuable 'information source' that helps to shape their self-identity than similar depictions in advertising.

The implications are not only important for media planners and marketing strategists trying to communicate with Millennials as consumers (see 'Outside Cool') but also to motivate and inspire them in the workplace.

Not that this is anything new. It just hasn't been fully acknowledged until recently. UK Indian entrepreneur G.K. Noon, for example, built a $40 million dollar business out of the demand in Europe for ready-made Indian food, working closely with large supermarket chains such as Waitrose and Sainsbury. The key to the success of his company has been his use of custom-built technology, which allows him to mass manufacture Indian food without sacrificing the quality that the supermarkets require.

What alumni are saying to us is 'tell me something that I didn't know I needed to know. Challenge me. Astonish me.' If the session is led by a well-known professor, they do not want well-polished presentations based on his well-polished theories. They want him to explore dangerous territory and ideas on the cutting edge, where they can make their own contribution to emerging concepts and be present while they emerge.

Caroline Buller, Cranfield School of Management

For example, to produce large quantities of the popular marinated dish, chicken tikka, he sourced and adapted German machinery that had previously been used to prepare commercially produced charcuterie. Noon believes that there will always be new technology of which he is currently unaware. 'I am not an engineer by profession, but I have an open and inquiring mind about food technology,' he says. 'If someone has a machine that will help me, I will travel the world to seek it out.'[10]

So how does he keep his enthusiasm for this quest alive? His source of inspiration is not just the example of his father, who started the Bombay-based sweet company that Noon used as a platform to set up in the UK. Film directors Steven Spielberg, James Cameron and Ridley Scott have also played their part.

Born and brought up in a country that is still the world's most prolific producer of films, Noon was movie-crazy from an early age. Despite his business and other commitments, he still goes to the cinema at least once every ten days. He is a cultured man with a strong interest in Indian classical music but he really unwinds by watching mass-market Hollywood blockbusters with high-tech special effects.

'The effects they achieve in films like *Gladiator, Titanic* or *Jurassic Park* fascinate me,' he says. 'I want to jump up and stop the movie mid-stream to find out how they achieve them. My conclusion as I exit the cinema is always to reflect that if the film industry can push out the boundaries of technology to keep their business fresh, so can I.'

The effects they achieve in films like Gladiator, Titanic *or* Jurassic Park *fascinate me. I want to jump up and stop the movie mid-stream to find out how they achieve them. My conclusion as I exit the cinema is always to reflect that if the film industry can push out the boundaries of technology to keep their business fresh, so can I.*

G.K. Noon,
Indian entrepreneur

Similarly, the pioneering general manager of product development at Virgin Atlantic in the 1990s, Chris Brady, traces his creativity back to his school days. Chris Brady had a strong interest at school in both the arts and science, but the rigid specialization required by sixth-form education made it difficult for him to pursue both. He opted for the sciences, taking an engineering degree sponsored by British Airways.

Joining the engineering group at Virgin Atlantic soon after he graduated, Brady has used his foundation in the sciences as a platform for a career in general management. In 1993, after working on the technical aspects of new product development in engineering, he transferred to the marketing department to launch the then new product development group. But being prevented from studying the arts still rankles.

'I was brought up by my mother and my aunt, which emphasized to me the importance of feminine relationships and also fuelled my interest in the arts,' he says. 'Yet I was also educated in a school run by priests whose approach was highly vocational. As a result I was pushed down the science path and not allowed to study art. This is not to say that I have not found my career unstimulating. I became an engineer because it suits my language and a desire to seek out the underlying "organizing" principle behind all aspects of life. But in recent years I have found that I have a strong aesthetic sense which informs my decisions at work and which has probably been fuelled by the frustration of not being able to do art at school.'

These two motivating forces have distilled into a strong interest in design and as general manager of product development, Brady has every opportunity to pursue it. 'I am not a designer but I now have the opportunity to simulate their approach and language. My job involves designing the uniforms, seats, pillows, napkins, cutlery and crockery that we use in the cabins as well as the technical systems and the content of the in-flight entertainment. It allows me to draw on both the physicist and the aesthetic in me and to apply both of these to the development and delivery of value added services.'

Brady's most important project to date has been supervizing the design of a new seat for Virgin Atlantic's business class cabins, an enterprise that has involved him in setting up a wholly-owned subsidiary of Virgin to undertake the design work, prior to the manufacturing process being contracted out to external suppliers.

The project, which arose out of a three-year collaboration with postgraduate students at the Royal College of Arts, has allowed Brady to draw on insights and analogies inspired by another private love of his – cars. He keeps abreast of the latest developments in car manufacture as a leisure interest and this is now proving invaluable in trying to break down the rigid thinking that still governs how aircraft seats are designed.

'Compared to the aircraft manufacturing industry, the automotive industry changes very rapidly,' he says. 'Changes to the cabin of the car take place year in and year out whereas aircraft cabins have remained relatively unchanged in the last decade. A further barrier to seat design is the mentality of the suppliers. Aircraft seat engineers have little or no contact with the customers who sit in their products. Their point of reference is the Boeing seat interface manual which talks about technical weight distribution and centres of gravity and not comfort, leg room and ease of access.'[11]

What people do outside work is therefore critical to their creativity at work. It guides their sense of what is possible and allows them to make those critical, previously unmade connections that lie at the heart of most breakthroughs in business thinking. This has always been the case but the wholly different work–life agenda of Millennials, the 24/7 dynamic described earlier, makes the possibilities that much easier to tap.

Pretty much every piece of academic research undertaken in the field of employee relationships in the past five years confirms this. London Business School's Sumantra Goshal, in his book *The Individualised Corporation*,[12] argues that corporations will have to examine more rigorously what they can offer a talented but footloose generation whose skills, creativity and dynamism they badly need. A new 'moral' contract should be based on respect for the individual as the source of most of the 'value added' that companies offer and, in the absence of any career assurance, corporations must accept responsibility for helping individuals realize their best potential.

This smacks of the concept of organizations offering 'employability' to their workers in place of employment security – a notion that was discredited in the 1990s in the wake of the turmoil caused by an almost continual round of mergers and industrial restructuring. But Goshal goes further than that. He subscribes to the idea of a 'third place', a source of fulfilment and self-expression separate from both workplace and home, somewhere in which people find their own independence and identity as individuals rather than as employees or family members.

As we already saw in the last chapter (see 'Balance'), this extends much further in Millennials than the relaxation that stems from socializing or clubbing. If companies can find ways of helping their staff combine their mainstream work with the 'third place' in their lives – offering work patterns or resources to help them run a parallel home-based business or band (see the example of Tom in 'The Provenance of Cool') or support, on company time, a cause they subscribe to (see the example of ConAgra in 'Outside Cool') – then, Goshal argues, they will have a recruitment and retention aid that will genuinely appeal to their Generation Y workers.

Similarly, the US employment researcher, Denise Rousseau, stresses the importance of any 'psychological contract' between an organization and an individual that requires the individual to bring emotional commitment to their work to encompass the 'whole person'. Contracts between employer and employee should 'connect' with the private life of the individual, and the sources of his or her own identity and self-esteem.[13]

The most popular way of doing this to date has been to encourage staff with the right skills and motivation to start up company-funded spin-off ventures. Incubating, as it is called, has become increasingly commonplace in the last decade.

Idealab, a pioneer California-based incubator of start-ups uses incubating methods to invent new businesses. The company's Pasadena headquarters operates in a 50,000 square foot one-storey building in which people are forced to run up against each other. Founder Bill Gross believes in 'cross-pollination' among everyone in the building. His own office is in the centre, with concentric rings of desks around it, those in the innermost circle belonging to employees working on early-stage start-ups. As the businesses develop, they move their desks further away from the centre. Once they achieve the critical mass of 70 employees, they leave and set up their own offices.

We keep saying that corporations should have a vision and a mission that should be about more than creating shareholder value – but I've yet to see many big companies create something that will really get people leaping out of bed.
Charles Handy,
UK business guru

Idealab also practices the fail-to-succeed philosophy, being prepared to invest in scores of potential businesses that flop in order to find a handful that will make it big. The company overreached itself with rash investments in 2000 that were scythed down in the dot.com massacre the following year, but it is still fizzing with ideas it claims will revolutionize the Internet.

Following similar principles, telecoms giant Nortel Networks set up in 1998 what they call an in-house incubator called the Business Ventures Group, which encourages staff to come to the organization with ideas for new start-ups and shepherds the ones they think have promise from inception to launch.[14]

Two of their Ottawa employees, Gord Larose and David Allan, came to Nortel with an idea they dreamed up over the kitchen table – renting software over the Internet. The service would allow people to sample programs in different ways: using a free trial offer, paying for a few hours of use, buying the software outright or renting to own.

Fours years later, the idea had evolved, with Nortel's help, into a full-blown company called Channelware. It has 60 employees and offices in Ottowa, New York, San Francisco and Los Angeles. Until recently, Nortel had a majority shareholding but they spun it off in 2000. Under the spin-off, Nortel now owns 44 per cent of the company, Channelware's employees own about 20 per cent and various other investors own the rest.

Larose and Allan were prepared to make the trade-off because Nortel's business venturing enabled them to test the idea out in a less risky atmosphere. 'Most of us are in big-company camps, whatever the newspapers tell us,' their vice-chairman recently commented.

Support from Nortel included:

- Infrastructure: Nortel helped out with office equipment, office-space leases and legal advice.
- A sounding board: Nortel are committed to hearing ideas, even if they are only partially formed – 'We let people refine their plans and pitch them to us again,' says a member of the group's advisory board, 'but you don't get a second chance with venture capitalists.'
- Help with prototyping: Nortel's technical experts worked with Larose and Allan to develop the software that enables Channelware to deliver its service to clients.
- Big-game endorsement: Larose and Allan claim that many of their largest customers would not have done business with them had Channelware not been a Nortel Network venture.

Joanne Hyland, who heads up Nortel's Business Ventures Group, points to this kind of support that helps the initiative create a win-win solution for the company and the start-up pioneers. New ventures do not just need an idea. As we will see in 'Managing Cool', they need a team, a secure environment and the financial support to shape and pilot the scheme. Most venture capitalists expect the initiative to work first time. Nortel give their budding entrepreneurs the 'space' and licence to experiment.

Finally, it is worth stressing that if you think working for your organization is challenging and worth taking time out for, you need to get the message across early – and the medium is as important as the message.

As we saw in 'The Provenance of Cool', the fact that anything between a third and a half of workers in Western economies now work part-time or from home means that Millennials will have less of an accurate picture of what corporate employment is like. Their parents will not conform to the stereotypical office workers of the past. In these circumstances, the limited picture that Millennials have of office life – picked up from ads, television, comic strips or, worse, the harrowing experiences of their own parents during a decade of redundancies and work-based stress – may hardly be a recommendation.

Twenty-year-old Katya and 17-year-old Max's early perceptions of work (see 'The Provenance of Cool') were almost wholly shaped by the way their parents worked. As their mother Carol explained during the interview: 'You got an almost incomprehensible stare from both of them when you asked what their first perceptions of office life were and this is because for almost all of their lives I was working from home running a one-person desktop publishing outfit where there was no staff and there was no boss. In addition, their father is a lecturer at a local university who also spent a lot of time at home and had almost complete control over his working schedule.'

Apart from the largely negative impression of work picked up from TV ads – like intense flu remedies that forced people to return to work before they were ready – the first 'real' impression of employment they received was on a work placement scheme organized by their respective schools. Each came out of the experience with very different impressions.

Because he showed an early aptitude for maths, Max was placed in a relatively unknown accountancy firm. Afterwards, he described the experience as 'the most boring two weeks of my life'. The office ran on highly traditional lines. Routine tasks and conventional command and control rules applied – so different from the way he saw his mother work at home and the 'chaotic' (aka self-managed) way he had seen his father work at college when he went visiting. Although there were young people in the department, everybody clock-watched and thought and acted along the same lines. It was exactly like characters depicted in *The Office*.

The humour, as office humour often is, was internally focused. It drew on reference points and 'targets' that presupposed you had worked in the place for years – whereas that of Max's was schoolboy and based on games, comics or programmes that most of the people in the department had neither seen nor heard of. When, out of a sense of frustration at the Orwellian regime he felt he had been dropped into, he created a screensaver for himself with the words 'Two plus two equals five', it was deemed highly inappropriate by his supervisor.

Critically, the manager that was supposed to supervise the placement was not there for the first two days. Max was left with no sense of what the work was all for. When the company was sufficiently impressed with him to let him undertake proper professional number crunching, he still found it unchallenging. Although he is very intellectually adroit, he comes from an inner-city school in Hackney, a London suburb that has a particularly black school performance record, and people made assumptions. 'I think they thought I came from a ghetto,' he said.

By contrast, Katya liked her work placement. In fairness, the work of the department – communications – was more interactive and engaging and the organization she worked for – the Royal Mail – is a household name with greater kudos. However, what really mattered to her was the attention that the organization paid to her personally.

'I enjoyed it,' she says. 'You had proper mentors. I didn't always enjoy being stuck with the filing but I did enjoy working with the woman who took me around to different departments and got the staff to talk to me so that I had a proper idea of what was going on. She also took me to an advertising agency because I had said I was interested in that. The guy there gave me a long presentation, which was a bit boring – you know, get real, I am only a schoolgirl really – but I was really impressed with the people they had done ads for. I think I was the first person the woman who was running things had been a mentor for, so she was really eager.' (She was in fact a graduate in her early 20s.)

Many of the points of good practice Royal Mail adopted – take a mentoring approach, use a manager who is young and closer to the visitor's culture, plan the whole placement to give the visitor the maximum exposure to all the activities of the firm/department, including external suppliers and/or clients, find out what the visitor wants and accommodate the request if at all possible – would not have looked out of place on the 'to do' list of a recruitment manager 30 years ago.

But as Cec, the mother from another family we interviewed, stressed, it is all the more important now. 'Both my children [James, 21, and Ruth, 18 – see 'The Provenance of Cool'] were unhappy at the way I was made redundant two years ago. Their image of the workplace was largely negative. Ruth's perceptions were also shaped by a school project with an advertising agency that showed her how much in-fighting there is inside most offices. What is really turning around my son's feelings is the fact that the company where he is currently working on a graduate intake is involving him in real work and enabling him to take decisions that will contribute to the firm's future.'

Technology certainly has a role to play here. In a concerted effort to understand what makes tomorrow's accountants tick, PriceWaterhouseCoopers in the US recently launched a recruiting website tailored specifically for Millennials (www.pwcglobal.com/lookhere).

The interactive 'flash-animated' site features Millennial-age recruits (none of whom would fit the buttoned-down stereotype of an accountant), video clips of company interns and associates discussing their jobs, and such site sections as 'Propel Your Career', 'Meet Great People', 'Get Cool Assignments', 'Make a Difference', and 'Balance Work and Life'.

The website, launched in February 2002, formed part of the larger campaign supported by advertising in 40 college newspapers. But the website, which got 55,000 hits in the first three months, was the centrepiece. In the words of Brent Inman, leader of the firm's US college recruiting, 'It's radio, TV, newspaper, entertainment, and information all rolled up into one.'

Its role as an interactive research medium – feeding PriceWaterhouseCoopers information about the attitudes and aspirations of likely candidates as well as projecting a 'cool' image of accountancy as a profession – was vitally important that year. The spring 2002 campaign came at a time when Arthur Andersen's involvement in the Enron scandal threatened to smear the image of other big accounting firms. Add that to a 20 per cent decline in the number of accounting majors in the previous five years, and drops of 50 to 60 per cent at top schools, and it is easy to see why PriceWaterhouseCoopers was looking for new ways to reach out.

'We believe passionately that we have to be visible and positive in the college market right now,' Robert Daugherty, US leader of human capital at the firm said at the time. 'It's essential that we communicate with students about the good things they'll find in our profession.'

FINDING A NEW 'HOW'

You only know what you can recall.
Walter Ong, author of *Orality and Literacy*

Making sure that this rich seam of experience and insight is teased out of them is dependent on the way day-to-day work is managed. The first change is in *how* it is conducted.

As the cyber-business fanzine *Fast Company* stresses, Millennials come to companies with their brains already out of the box and the priority should be to keep it there rather than doing everything possible to paint them into a corner. Yet the professions that most fed management theory and concepts in the twentieth century – accountancy, law, engineering – are heavily steeped in the scientific principle that there is a 'right' and a 'wrong' way of doing everything.

The physicist turned management guru Danah Zohar believes that most senior managers are trapped in a 'Newtonian' view of the world which states that all things are simple, law abiding and ultimately controllable – when they should base their perspective on the laws of quantum physics which state that all things are complex, chaotic and uncertain. As a result, she argues, too many management decisions are based on the idea that there is one best way forward rather than the concept that there are many paths to any chosen goal.[15]

By contrast, people who have not been imbued with this kind of professional orthodoxy, including the Millennial generation new to business, are more open to diversity. Like Ricardo Semler (see 'Cool Leadership'), they have a greater tendency to ask 'why' and seek fundamental answers; and have the capacity to face and use adversity. They actively seek uncomfortable situations because they recognize that their ability to interpret the environment around them will be enhanced as a result.

This is as important in day-to-day decision-making as it is in shaping high company strategy. Creative discussions and problem-solving exercises are dominated by the idea that you do not volunteer any contribution that has not been thought through or supported by a rational argument. Yet proponents of lateral thinking, such as Alex Osborne in the 1960s or Edward De Bono in the following two dec-ades, stress that this form of censorship – by colleagues or the individual originating the thought – is guaranteed to discourage 'out of the box' thinking.

Osborne in particular stresses that it is not the quality of thoughts that matter but the volume. Wild unworkable ideas act as bridge to insights that are more practical. These insights will not be reached without the change in perspec-tive that the wilder thoughts bring with them. The purpose of any creative discussion should be to encourage all par-ticipants to say, literally and with the licence of others in the group, the first thing that comes into their minds.[16]

This requires trust, confidence and no fear of ridicule. In a truly creative exchange, Osborne argues, everyone should suspend judgement. Anything goes – there is no *wrong* idea. Once the idea is expressed, it should not be held on to by the individual who originated it. Participants should build on each other's ideas, abandoning any attempt to 'own' or protect any idea that emerges.

Ironically, establishing this 'anything goes' environment requires a few rules to be obeyed. In 'Brainstorming Cool', we set out the most important, based on Osborne's principles of brainstorming, together with a number of 'warm-up' exercises that will help teams and groups get into the right spirit.

It also requires the right management culture to underpin it. Few companies, for example, practice brainstorming more enthusiastically than IDEO, an industrial design company. Founded by David Kelley in 1978 and based in Palo Alto, IDEO has launched a stunningly diverse range of products, from the Polaroid I-Zone Camera to Crest Toothpaste's Neat Squeeze tube.

At IDEO, the rules of brainstorming are strictly observed. Design teams are expected to make mistakes early and often. Coming to the 'right' solution too quickly is discouraged. Team members are encouraged to question any and all assumptions about what innovation means. At IDEO, people are not deemed to be innovative unless they are challenging the client's, the team's and their own preexisting notions.

Paradoxically this means that during brainstorms, any notions other than standard company or industry orthodoxies are given an open hearing. David Kelley argues that innovation is not just about surprising ideas. It is about surprising people – and that fostering innovation is mainly about encouraging people to relate to each other in creative ways. 'Being a design genius is great,' he concludes. 'Being a design genius at the expense of the team is not.'[17]

This brings us to the central issue of good team leadership. Effective team leaders in the front line are important for two reasons. First, at a time when loyalty to an anonymous corporate entity, however well 'branded', is at an all-time low, whether or not a talented individual stays with the organization is often determined by the quality of leadership they encounter face to face.

Millennials enter the workforce with an exceptionally jaded view of the corporates. Sam (see 'The Provenance of Cool') moved from one organization to another until she found a boss she got on with. 'If you have crappy bosses belittling you the whole time, making you feel worthless, you are not going to work hard for them. I work for a boss now, and he is the first, that makes me feel really valued. I want to work hard for him. I would rather be at home otherwise.'

Secondly, effective leadership is all the more important if the team is virtual. A survey of 371 managers by the UK-based management centre the Roffey Park Institute found that nearly half (46 per cent) currently worked in virtual teams and over three-quarters (80 per cent) claimed that virtual management arrangements had increased in their organization in the past five years.[18]

Researchers Andy Smith and Annette Sinclair found, however, that virtual management is very difficult to do well. 'Because of the reduced face-to-face contact and separation from co-workers, it is often more difficult to establish and maintain trust between members,' they stress. 'Technology can be both an aid and a barrier to effective communication. Sometimes it creates misunderstanding because you lose the nuances of facial expressions and body language which enhance face-to-face contact.'

As a result, they conclude, managers need well-honed interpersonal and communication skills, as well as integrity, clarity of direction and an ability to influence others and generate trust and productivity in the team. Other qualities include an ability to build and maintain relationships, a participative management style and good links with the wider organization.

As IDEO's work philosophy illustrates, effective team leaders have the ability to champion and foster creativity in others. Our own research into innovation – also undertaken for Roffey Park, with organizations as varied as a major airline, an international aid organization, a fast-growth enterprise, a teaching hospital and a dot.com start-up – suggests that the major challenge facing all these firms is not a lack of innovative thought on the ground but the inability or unwillingness of front-line project managers or team leaders to spot the idea's potential, foster it and win the resources to 'make it real' (see 'Brainstorming Cool').[19]

If you have crappy bosses belittling you the whole time, making you feel worthless, you are not going to work hard for them. I work for a boss now, and he is the first, that makes me feel really valued. I want to work hard for him. I would rather be at home otherwise.

Sam

The ability of a team leader to search for and unlock hidden potential is therefore more important than imposing method or keeping to pre-set targets. As Chris Byron, one of the key project leaders in British Airway's construction of its state-of-the-art Waterside headquarters, describes: 'We did not work to a rigid timescale. I did not try to drive things through like a professional chairman because railroading of this kind leaves a lack of real consensus that has a habit of jumping back at you further down the line. There were too many people with too many strong views and vested interests. Consequently, I adopted a more facilitating style, giving everyone a nominal time of five minutes to stress what issues they felt were at stake.

'Of course everyone took more time – up to fifteen minutes in many cases – but I was prepared to let the discussion go on if it contributed to our collective perspective. Obviously I had to pull things together and ultimately make a decision but taking the time and patience to listen to the issues, sometimes for longer than I really wanted to, helps to create a common language in a team made up from very disparate backgrounds and disciplines.'

> *Obviously I had to pull things together and ultimately make a decision but taking the time and patience to listen to the issues, sometimes for longer than I really wanted to, helps to create a common language in a team made up from very disparate backgrounds and disciplines.*
>
> Chris Byron, British Airways project leader, 1997

FINDING A NEW 'WHERE'

> *The 'online' self is supported by neither time, space nor body, and yet it is unmistakably present.*
>
> From a Mintel website

The second change is in *where* work is conducted. Millennials live a 24/7 life and the work they undertake for any one employer is likely to fit into a wider tapestry of activity.

This is important for two reasons. The first is that Millennials no longer think 'careers'. 'Career is important but it is not the dominant force it used to be,' says Keith Dugdale, director of recruitment and resourcing at the management consultancy KPMG. 'There is a shift from a job-for-life mentality to self-management of careers. Millennial-age graduates want a job to meet their values and needs as well as to pay their mortgage. They want to know how they will be stretched as individuals and if they will be able to strike a work–life balance.'

'We have to think about people and be smarter about career development,' adds Ros King, managing director of advertising agency J. Walter Thompson. 'It's about getting work to fit into people's lives and not the other way around.'[20]

Secondly, being more flexible about 'where' and 'when' staff undertake their work is not just a matter of retaining their loyalty by redesigning work to fit in with the Millennial 24/7 lifestyle. In an age when knowledge work makes up between half and three-quarters of the output underpinning commercial profitability (see 'Cool Beginnings'), it enables people to work smarter rather than harder.

A survey of Australia's leading scientific research organization CSIRO by Dr Cathy Sheehan of the University of Tasmania found that there was a direct trade-off between the amount of 'reflection time' and the originality of the work undertaken by front-line researchers.[21]

'Once upon a time the scientists here were encouraged to take 30 per cent of their time off to just think,' remarked one senior research fellow. 'We just don't have the time to do that any more. Obviously the pressures to be accountable makes that no longer possible and I can certainly see the need to be more focused. But at the same time, a lot of creative thinking time and output is lost.'

Nor is this equation confined to highly cerebral research work. Our own research on how ideas are inspired in individuals (see 'Managing Millennials') found that the best ideas in employees of any age are, in any case, mostly triggered well away from the office – in a car to and from work, in the shower, while waking up or going to sleep – in an atmosphere or 'space' where they can 'drift and dream' their way around the subject.

The underlying principle behind the design of British Airways' headquarters at Heathrow is to create an 'office-less' working culture where work can be conducted anywhere, underpinned by a virtual management information system that enables managers to call in or phone in to update themselves with events. Although the new way of working took time to be accepted by older staff (see 'Managing Cool'), it was taken up with alacrity in the departments with a high proportion of Generation X workers.[22]

A good example is the relationship marketing department, which runs the air miles and other customer loyalty service schemes. The essential elements of the job are conducted off-site and people only need to check in to the office from time to time to pick up messages. Work in these circumstances is conducted anywhere. Staff can work from home as often as they like so long as they keep in touch and meet their targets. The location and timing of meetings is all subject to negotiation between team or project members rather than being laid down from the top. According to Jackie, the HR strategist who piloted the scheme, this level of freedom is seen as a huge motivator among Generation X staff, as opposed to older staff who often still see it as a threat.

The freedom for staff to meet, conduct company business and interact where and when they like, subject only to meeting their targets, is the central tenet of work in the Brazilian engineering giant Semco – described by the chief executive Ricardo Semler in his 2003 book *The Seven Day Weekend*.[23] The underlying philosophy behind the title is that work should be made as enjoyable as leisure so that companies can tap into the creative energy that many employees focus on in their private pursuits and do not always bring to their work (see 'Cool Leadership'). For example, Semler found that one of the reasons why many workers liked working at home was because they could rest in the middle of the day, to recoup their energies. So he introduced the right to 'catnap' on company premises and provided facilities where they could do this – and saw an immediate boost in work unit performance rates.

'What is important is treating your employees like adults,' Semler stresses. 'This means learning to relinquish control and allowing other people to make decisions. Giving in on issues like flexible working does not mean giving up on productivity. We don't see an adversarial relationship between quality of life and work and, in an industry like manufacturing, you have to always question whether there is a more intelligent way to work. Someone who works five hours a day might perform better than someone who does ten, particularly when what they are bringing to the job is insight and lateral thinking.'

Semler's insight – that people often bring more creativity and energy to their leisure than their work – is not new. Ten years ago, British Petroleum ran a seminal careers workshop for middle-level executives who were 'deemed' to be grounded. They found that far from being less talented than managers on the fast track, they were in fact more innovative. They helped their spouses run home-based businesses, were talented local councillors, school governors or charity trustees and had fascinating hobbies. They just didn't bring this talent to work with them.

For Millennials with a 24/7 life agenda, this is a key issue. Tom (see 'The Provenance of Cool') combines award-winning website design work and playing bass in a band that is enjoying great popularity playing the London club and pub circuit. The first activity is in the daytime, the second in the evening. Much time in his role with the band is spent in transit and links with clients are often made by mobile phone. 'So long as the contact is made and the work is good, nobody complains,' he says. 'How I conduct the work is a critical issue. Where I conduct it isn't.'

His girlfriend Sophie, who works as a fashion assistant at a leading monthly magazine, argues that if employers really want their staff to work all hours of the day, then they have to be prepared to offer maximum flexibility in where and when it is conducted. 'If there are no boundaries any more then the benefits have to stretch both ways,' she says. 'The freedom to work from home and combine what I am doing for my employer with what I am doing elsewhere, so long as I meet my deadlines and objectives, is going to become really essential.'

Tom argues that even the most interactive and complex tasks can be conducted at a distance using Internet technology. The constraint in the past decade has rarely been the possible applications of the software coming on to the market. Rather, it has been the 'comfort factor' of the people using it. Since the single defining characteristic of Millennials is that they have been using Internet and mobile phone technology to communicate and interact with their own self-made community, this is not going to prove a constraint in their case.

> *What is important is treating your employees like adults This means learning to relinquish control and allowing other people to make decisions. Giving in on issues like flexible working does not mean giving up on productivity. Someone who works five hours a day might perform better than someone who does ten, particularly when what they are bringing to the job is insight and lateral thinking.*
>
> Ricardo Semler, chairman and chief executive, Semco

Recent tests of new software designed to support electronic brainstorming by researchers at the Massachusetts Institute of Technology, involving 800 people, found that the creative output from electronic brainstorming sessions was greater than those conducted face to face – and that, furthermore, these productivity gains increased along with

If there are no boundaries any more then the benefits have to stretch both ways. The freedom to work from home and combine what I am doing for my employer with what I am doing elsewhere, so long as I meet my deadlines and objectives, is going to become really essential.

Sophie

the size of group.[24] This was because in face-to-face sessions, the most assertive and outgoing members of the group dominated the exchange, with quieter but equally insightful individuals keeping their thoughts to themselves. But whereas pre-Millennial workers are often constrained by the fact that they never used the medium in their personal lives to bond or interact intimately with friends, it is second nature to teenagers and twentysomethings.

Similarly, global companies in the 1990s found that it was possible to conduct highly sophisticated management development exercises at a distance, using the latest conferencing and intranet systems, which previously would have only been possible in the classroom (see Table 4.1).

A good example is the international in-company MBA programme run by Henley Management College for Standard Chartered Bank (also explored in the next chapter). In the first intake, in 1991, 18 managers from 12 countries took part, ranging from the chief financial officer in Tokyo and the senior strategic officer in Hong Kong to branch managers in Sidcup, UK, and Kuala Lumpur, Malaysia.[25]

Participants were provided with a laptop computer to help them communicate with each other, their tutors and in-company trainers through Henley's global conferencing system. All academic materials, background reading, individual assignments and group tasks undertaken by a series of study groups, to which all participants were assigned, were conducted using this medium.

Table 4.1 Three generations of e-learning technology and their impact

Technology	Characteristics
First generation	Instructor driven, and simply understood as e-training: traditional courses and text put online and typically organized in a linear fashion
Second generation	Learner driven, self-organizing and evolving, and capable of being accessed at any point for 'just in time' learning and 'as needed' basis; simply understood as e-learning, but using today's limited range of Internet media and so delivering a narrow range of sensory stimulation and interactive capabilities
Third generation	Learner driven, built on 'second-generation' broadband platform with advanced interactive technology using a full range of media giving a richly interactive experience, with text, voice, pictures and movement delivered across the Net – requiring more advanced software and bandwidth than most have today
The e-impact	*2001 corporate reality*
• Cost reduction	– being achieved frequently
• Improved accessibility	– as above
• Increased quality	– not there yet, in many cases
• Personal, collaborative learning at a distance	– just beginning

Source: Professor Gareth Morgan, York University, Toronto, 2001

'The Holy Grail for us was to bring about an imaginative interaction between participants which leads to effective problem solving, decision making and the development of new ideas,' says Dominic Swords, the designer of the programme. 'New technologies such as groupware, discussion databases and the Internet increase the sense of intimacy between ourselves and the participants. They have replaced more bureaucratic forms of communication which have made it hard to maintain the sharing process when participants are dispersed in different parts of the world.'

A critical constraint to the design, however, was the assumption that the team spirit essential for the group exercises could only be established face to face – and that it was only once this bonding had been established by people eyeballing each other that the distance learning dynamic could kick in.

Consequently, residential seminars brought the group together once a year in Hong Kong, Kuala Lumpur and the UK. Each study group also met at least once a quarter. Dominic Swords stressed in 1997 that the degree of intimacy participants sustained over the Internet was possible only because of the ties that were made during these residential courses. 'The lesson we are learning again and again is that sophisticated learning over the Web can only be fostered through a face-to-face encounter.'

In the same way as team-based brainstorming, this may still be true of pre-Millennial generations, but not with people recruited straight from school or college.

FINDING A NEW 'WHAT'

One of the striking things about a virtual world system in which you have the ability to change the content of the world is that the distinction between your own body and the rest of the world is slippery.
Jaron Lanier, virtual reality designer

All of this presupposes that the Millennials employers recruit are allowed to use Internet and intranet technology in the way they are used to – that is, in a totally uninhibited, freestanding manner.

Unhappily this is not the case in all but a very small minority of companies. The policing of emails, facilitated by software that enables employers to 'sweep' all incoming messages for words and images they deem 'inappropriate' has become well nigh universal over the last decade, prompting surprisingly little media debate. Even taking aside the human and employment rights issues this level of intrusion incurs, it has turned email and intranet exchanges from one of the most liberating mediums of this generation to an Orwellian nightmare that undermines both enthusiasm and creativity in how day-to-day work is conducted.

The success of electronic brainstorming uncovered by MIT (see above) was not only because discussions took place on a more level playing field, allowing less assertive group members to contribute their insights without being drowned out by other voices. Email and intranet exchanges add something more than that – at least potentially. People who use them interactively tend to use the same language, syntax and 'turn of phrase' as if they were chatting to each other. They do not filter or censor their thoughts in the way that they would if they were composing a letter or writing a report.

As a consequence, the idiom, metaphor or 'verbal' emphasis that is often sanitized out of written business exchanges, and which inspires new insights or ideas, is captured in a way that rarely occurs on flipcharts or through the subjective filter of other participants' memories.

The key thing here is that people do not have to *watch what they say*, as long as trust has been established between them. Our own work on innovation for the Roffey Park Institute[26] suggests that this is the single most important factor in 'no holds barred' creativity; and that it produces a stream of new ideas uncluttered by thoughts such as 'I shouldn't say this because it might offend someone' or 'I shouldn't say this because I can't substantiate it.'

With the advent of email and intranet screening comes another thought: 'I shouldn't say this because someone outside the conversation, whom I don't know, might disapprove.' Swearing is a case in point. The use of bad language, even of the 'fuck, fuck fuckity-fuck' variety, may be highly inappropriate in the case of a client presentation when nobody knows each other and the 'rules of the game' governing business interchanges have not yet been established.

Between individuals in a creative group that have worked together for months, or between clients and long-standing suppliers, it can often denote trust. But this frankness, one of the most important contributions to creativity, is contextual. If individuals suspect that someone else is listening in on their conversation – and screening emails amounts to this, even if it is not intended – then their spontaneity will be immediately diminished, if not destroyed.

Of course, no decent team leader would sanction such language if they knew it would offend a colleague, let alone a client. But the fact is that most of us use 'bad' language casually in casual business exchanges at some point. Even if we don't use it at work, we certainly do at home. Among teenagers and twentysomethings brought up on books and films such as *Trainspotting* and *Pulp Fiction*, it is commonplace. If companies block or ban certain words in all circumstances on the grounds that, as one executive put it, 'We don't want these sorts of word associated with our firm,' their younger staff will deem them total prats. They won't say it. But they'll think it.

In summary, there are good legal reasons why email or intranet exchanges cannot be completely unregulated – the downloading of pornography or the use of electronic exchanges for company fraud are two good examples. But the methods used by many employers to police the Net – based on the prohibition of specific words or phrases – are, frankly, ludicrous and send out unintended signals to their staff that they are nothing more than prurient control freaks.

A journalist friend of ours recently had an article artificially refused by a magazine because she referred to the TV hit series *Sex in the City* and the screening software objected to the word 'sex'. Similarly, a research colleague recently conducted a serious study into HIV and medical screening and found he couldn't save reports on his computer filing system using the words 'HIV' or 'AIDS' because these were 'unauthorized' words. His contempt for his employer after that was all too evident, and he left for a competitor a few weeks later.

The issue of intranet policing is part of a larger dilemma: whether the system of language used by the organization is a turn-on or a turn-off to Millennials. As we highlighted in 'The Provenance of Cool', language – in terms of both vocabulary and usage – is a central dynamic of the Millennial culture. It is the conduit for Millennials' creative energy. In Millennial-targeted books, films, rap music and computer games, lingual anarchy reigns. There are no rules about how language should be used. It lives. Its influence on pre-Millennial culture is already being felt and the *legitimacy* of this *fait accompli* was recognized by the bible of English usage, the *Oxford Dictionary*, when it began publishing its New Words supplements in the early 1990s.

The idea that the language used in an organization directly affects its perspective of the world is not new. It was recognized two decades ago by etymologist Professor Johaan Roos of the International Institute for Management Development (IMD) in Lausanne, in his study of organizations such as Nestlé, IBM and Lufthansa.

Roos argues that an organization's ability to update and adapt its internal language is directly related to its ability to change. If the language is alive and vibrant, responding to the influx of new ideas and people, the outlook it helps to shape will keep the organization alive to the events around it. If it is stultified, jargon-ridden and shaped only by senior executives, so too will be the culture.[27]

A good illustration is poor report writing, where the vibrancy of what is going on in the front line is stultified by middle management caveats and rationalizations. Back in the mid-1990s Gordon Shaw, the executive director of planning at 3M – one of the most innovative companies in the world, with inventions such as microreplication-based abrasives and Post-It Notes to its credit – gradually became aware that the strategy of the company was not reflecting the inventive dynamism that was happening in its creative teams. They were, according to him, 'usually just lists of good things to do' that made 3M functionally stronger but failed to explain the logic or inspiration behind the strategy.

Shaw began to suspect that the style in which reports were written was a big part of the problem. In particular, like all reports written by senior managers, they used bullet points as a shorthand to summarize key points. This might fit in well with the 'cut to the quick' nature of boardroom business but it also 'dumbed down' the vitality or originality of what was being discussed.

Bullet points, in classic Newtonian style, reduce business arguments to its bare essentials and the choices available to the board to a series of 'either-or' choices. The rich detail of 'who did what and why' and the complexities of experimentation and exploration that led to new products being developed was completely exorcized, cutting top managers off from the gloriously messy and untidy process of invention that provided 3M with its profits.

Shaw decided that future boardroom reports at 3M should be written as proper stories. He turned to an article in *Scientific American* written by cognitive scientist William Calvin about how children learn about life from fantasy and also how college students learn about business in magazines such as *Time* and *Newsweek*.[28]

With this in mind, he set about encouraging all strategic planning sessions to be based on reports written as narrative stories rather than in bullet points. Here is an extract from the guidelines he issued to executives asked to contribute to planning sessions:

> *Planning by narrative is a lot like traditional storytelling. Like a good storyteller, the strategic planner needs to set the stage – defining the current situation in an insightful coherent manner. It also involves defining basic tensions and relationships: Which capabilities do we have and which do other players have? What do we believe the other players intend to do? How do key success factors compare with those of our competitors?*
>
> *Next, the strategic planner must introduce the dramatic conflict. What challenges does the company face in this situation? What critical issues stand as obstacles to success? ... Finally, a story must reach a resolution in a satisfying, convincing manner. The conclusion requires a logical, concise argument that is specific to the situation and leads to the desired outcome.*

It may seem extraordinary that companies like 3M should have invested this amount of time and effort in a campaign to change the way executives communicate with their staff and reflect their views. But 3M's Shaw insists that fostering the culture the company inherited from its founders while keeping its management practices up to date is one of the reasons for its success – because it shapes the way it sees itself and explains itself to its key workers.

Yet most organizations do not do this. They spend thousands, and in the case of the blue chips millions, hiring advertising or marketing agencies to pore over every

We keep saying that corpora-tions should have a vision and a mission that should be about more than creating sharehold-er value – but I've yet to see many big companies create something that will really get people leaping out of bed.
Charles Handy,
UK business guru

word, every phrase and metaphor and every external image seen by their potential customers. At the same time, they care little about the language that is used in the work-force unless it is likely to get them in trouble with the law. Senior manag-ers often use second-hand clichés to explain the company's objectives and values that bear little relation to the reality on the ground.

SUMMARY

Perfection can only be accomplished by using old knowledge in new ways.
Robert Sutton, Professor of Science of
Technology, Stanford University

Reviewing how employers best respond to the challenge of attracting and keeping a new generation of independent baggage-free and unsettled workers, it becomes clear that many of the strategies consist of measures that they should be doing anyway – only better.

They include:

- Introducing ideas-generation and team-working meth-ods that will mentally engage Millennials with bright ideas and keep them that way.
- Making spotting and championing good ideas among their staff an essential management role – one that is built into their job specification and that they are ap-praised by.

- Taking advantage of Millennials' comfort with Internet-based technology by introducing maximum flexibility in where work is undertaken – something that will also help them reconcile and integrate the work they undertake for the organization with their broader 24/7 lives.
- Ridding intranet and incoming Internet exchanges of the kind of policing that will undermine the very spontaneity and uninhibitedness that Millennials are best able to offer.
- Reviewing the way employee communications and strategy reporting is undertaken to ensure that it is up to date and reflects the reality on the ground.
- Helping individuals link work with the organization with other 'third place' activities that provide them with sources of self-fulfilment and self-expression – including supporting charitable causes on company time, offering imaginative patterns of work and offering the opportunity to help launch company-funded enterprise spin-offs.

Most of the existing literature on employing Millennials focuses on the cosmetic overlay: introducing an 'anything goes' dress code or mid-afternoon hockey or video games. But the real heart of the challenge is using the energy and independent spirit of Millennials to free up the whole organization. As Britain's premier management philosopher, Charles Handy comments: 'We keep saying that corporations should have a vision and a mission that should be about more than creating shareholder value – but I've yet to see many big companies create something that will really get people leaping out of bed.'

CRUX

5

Many of the attitudes and characteristics of Millennials are likely to change over time. They may be deferring some of the baggage of adult life – marriage or committed co-habitation, parenthood, property ownership – later than their parents or elder siblings. But these aspirations are still there. They may have little or no faith in the traditional altars of social security – a lifetime job or a safe pension – but they will find some way of putting resources aside for their old age.

But there are some beliefs and behaviours from their childhood that are not likely to change and which have disturbing implications for current business practice. This chapter deals with three of the most important.

ISSUE 1

Millennials have grown up more actively engaged in the shaping and execution of public policy than any previous generation. How is this likely to influence thinking on the purpose and parameters of global trade and international business management?

If we want to develop adults who are good citizens and good leaders, why encourage children to be neither?
Craig Kielberger founder, Free the Children

There never was an era when teenagers and young adults grew up more actively engaged in public policy. Involving young people in decision making – youth engage-ment as it is called – is a rising trend in the rich democratic world. In 2000, Carrie McDougall, a 22-year-old Australian, was chosen as a member of her country's delegation to the UN General Assembly. Fifteen other countries emulate this approach, delegations from Finland having done so since the UN's early days. Young people also form the majority on a number of the UN committees, most notably those considering issues surrounding environmental issues and the exploration of outer space.

This level of engagement reflects the early involvement of young people in decisions that directly affect them that starts in primary school and flows consistently through to more traditional active student union activity at college and beyond to direct involvement in local government. In Ontario, almost every high school has an elected school council, handling school-level issues. Once a year, the council leaders of some area assemble to elect the area's representative to the Ontario Secondary School Students' Association. Funded in part by the Ontario government, this body meets provincial officials and lobbies on province-wide issues. Recently it helped the Ontario government to legislate to require school boards – the elected bodies running the schools of a given area – to include one elected student. The student cannot vote and is excluded from some issues, such as hiring and firing, but otherwise is on a par with other members.[1]

Similarly, the New Zealand city of Wellington has a youth council that provides input to its policy making. Many schools and most universities in the city involve students in decision making, whether through informal meetings with principals or an elected seat of the university's board of governors. These young members often serve for shorter periods than others, typically for one year, and usually with pared down roles. Often they are barred from voting, especially if they are sitting on a board with elected officials. But their influence is felt through well-informed and supported argument forged in collaboration with teachers, parents and local politicians.[2]

Perhaps no one individual symbolizes the youth engagement movement more than Craig Kielberger. At the age of 12, sitting in his Toronto home, he read of a Pakistani boy speaking out against child labour. He went to see for himself and on his return founded an organization called Free the Children to protest and actively campaign for its abolition.

Now consulted regularly on the involvement of young people in public policy making, he argues that prosperous countries suffer from 'affluenza'. Children in poor countries are given too much responsibility, particularly in propping up their family and often on a subsistence-level income. Children in rich countries, by contrast, are either patronized or, if they do become actively involved in protest politics, denigrated.

Kielberger likes to compare his movement to those of women a century ago. They too were much talked about but seldom consulted, being viewed as unready for public responsibility. Today this seems ludicrous. But, Kielberger stresses, bodies such as UNICEF often discuss children's issues without including young people, let alone children, in their deliberations.[3]

The legacy of Millennials' early exposure to public policy issues is likely to be lifelong and deeply rooted. It could extend well beyond current concerns about corporate governance in the wake of the Enron and WorldCom scandals, or global environment resource management in the wake of the North–South divide.

Let's look at how it might apply to the issue that engaged Craig Kielberger when he was 12 – the use of child labour. The perspective of the current generation of Western-trained managers is that business operates best in an environment where it is not used as an instrument of state policy, where its ultimate accountability is to its shareholders and where the company's workforce, local or global, is a flexible resource subordinate to the declared interests of its own strategy rather than those of the community in which it operates. Yet they increasingly encounter countries, cultures and economic systems that reject or at least question these assumptions.

Western managers are largely brought up in a Christian culture that presupposes that child labour and indenture (i.e. slavery) are moral wrongs, that equality of opportunity (whether in terms of sex, race or religion) is a natural or 'God-given' human right and that meritocracy is the only arbiter of promotion and career advancement. These values inform and underpin the policies they apply to their worldwide operations, in the recruitment and development of its own workforce and in their selection of suppliers, distributors and commercial partners. Yet they increasingly encounter and, through these policies, determine the interests of societies that do not accept these apparent 'truths' and which are economically dependent on practices that they, the managers, find abhorrent.

This is not a temporary state of affairs. Experience in the early years of globalism in the early 1990s suggests that the gap in values and assumptions between the industrial and developing economies becomes more complex as levels of prosperity and education increase, enabling local countries and workforces to become partners rather than dependents.

As Robert Cooper, former head of policy planning at the British and Commonwealth Office, commented in a presentation to the World Trade Organization at its Davos conference in 1997:

> *In a situation where international businesses rather than nation states are shaping the post-industrial, post-modern world, the battles of tomorrow between states will be about whose industrial standards and corporate values will achieve global acceptance. The development of a stable democratic state requires the existence of an educated middle class. This is, and always has been, the product of the private sector. Eventually, successful states will be based on successful firms. This places the role of managers on a completely different plane.[4]*

In a current campaign to eradicate child labour worldwide, a number of sporting goods companies in the USA – including Nike, Reebok and Adidas – reached an agreement at the end of the last decade prohibiting the employment of children in suppliers manufacturing footballs, following reports that in India children as young as seven were involved in the process. When Nike was caught with its pants down soon after (see 'Outside Cool'), the damage to its brand image was immense.

It is difficult to argue against the abolition of child labour in as speedy a fashion as is practicable. But similar Western-led campaigns highlight the hazy ethical issues this kind of moral high ground can lead to. Environmentalists campaigning against the deforestation of Latin America or ivory poachers in Africa and politicians who attempt to eliminate the poppy growing industry in south-east Asia all face the same dilemma. Their actions benefit a wider world community but unless a substitute source of income is established, they deprive local communities of a vital source of income.

So in the case of the sports and clothes manufacturers, a Millennial-age agenda on international corporate social policy might raise questions not only about what will happen to children who should benefit from a proper education but also how local communities dependant on income from child labour will replace that income if it is taken away by a ban imposed by senior executives in a boardroom thousands of miles away. To do anything else is to place the opinions of stakeholders at home – who possess a real influence over the financial fortunes of the company through their investment and consumer power – over the interests of another set of stakeholders in the developing world whose poverty means they have no influence on the company's decisions at all.

Nor could it stop there. In the wake of the rapid expansion of Western companies into previously unexploited markets in Russia, China and India following the collapse or reform of Communist economies in the early 1990s, the UN started to raise issues about how this level of overseas investment should be managed to benefit local countries rather than undermine them (see box below). The UN agenda informed and inspired moderate opinion among the protestors at meetings of the World Trade Organization and the G8 countries at Seattle, Bologna and Davos.

However, the willingness of companies to fully subscribe to these principals remains spotty, and the case for them is at odds with the turnaround culture that motivated early global trade expansion.

In 1989 the US energy giant General Electric, for example, acquired a half-share of Tungsram, the Hungarian light-bulb manufacturer, at that time the fifth largest in Europe. It marked the first stage in what became an attempt by GE to build a Europe-wide lighting conglomerate following similar acquisitions in Italy, Scandinavia and the UK.

UN GUIDELINES ON INTERNATIONAL
INVESTMENT

Principles include:

- refraining, or continuing to refrain, from interference in purely domestic affairs;
- making deliberate efforts to ensure that company strategies and operations are fully consistent with the local nation's objectives and policies;
- showing flexibility in dealing with requests for local participation in ownership and control;
- bringing in capital from abroad, rather than pre-empting local financial resources;
- effectively transferring technologies adapted to local conditions and opportunities, and contributing to human resource development and investment in sound infrastructure;
- maximizing the utilization of local labour and other inputs, and permitting local participation in the capital and management of local affiliates;
- promoting export capacity and, as appropriate, efficient substitution for imports;
- abstaining from tax evasion and abusive transfer pricing;
- behaving in general as good corporate citizens.

Source: UN Conference on Trade and Development 1994

When Tungsram's Eastern European market disintegrated following the collapse the Comecon system, GE took it over completely and spent the next four years turning it around. Buying out the company's principal minority shareholder, the Hungarian Credit Bank, GE disinvested from Tungsram's loss-making subsidiaries. This, combined with the emergency measures needed to offset a record $105 million loss in 1992, resulted in half of Tungsram's workforce – slightly less than 9000 people – being laid off.[5]

In strict commercial terms the strategy worked. Injecting an investment of $600 million, GE turned a $105 million loss in 1992 into a working profit by 1994, creating 1400 jobs and providing valuable retraining for much of the remaining workforce. However, the political fallout of GE's tough love approach was considerable. The reformist government that initially approved GE's investment was replaced in May 1995 by one made up of pre-1989 socialists.

Whose rights and wishes should have predominated here? GE's tough restructuring programme was vindicated by the turnaround of Tungsram into a viable business. In economic terms it was fully justified to take the action it did. Indeed, the turnaround of Tungsram by GE is used by some business schools as a model case study on its MBA and executive programmes. But in the process, the company rode roughshod over the wishes and interests of minority shareholders, trade unions and local public opinion, adding to the difficulties of a severely embattled national government and (arguably) contributing to its downfall.

GE's experience is not unique. Its decisions were justified by the commercial outcome. But its experiences in Hungary, together with those of LS&C in Asia, illustrate the near impossibility of conducting a uniform social policy in every community in the world where multinationals are active. Corporate governance systems that still rely on nineteenth-century limited liability legislation make it impossible to produce concepts of stakeholder management that are anything other than an affectation. A Millennial-age agenda might conclude that these concerns warrant undertakings by global companies that are binding in international law.

ISSUE 2

Internet and third-generation mobile phone technology is transforming the way ideas and their creative output are disseminated, on a scale that has not been seen since the invention of the printing press. Social and commercial innovation has profited from this but the measures currently in place to protect its long-term financial returns have been fatally undermined in the process. How can the international business community respond to Millennials' rejection of contemporary intellectual property rights?

Technology, putting it bluntly, has made piracy and plagiary easier – and less morally troubling to many people, particularly Millennials, in the process.

Property is theft
Proudhon,
early nineteenth-century
father of anarchism

The 'cut and paste' facility on office software has made it possible to lift whole paragraphs of other people's intellectual work in a matter of seconds. The consequences were illustrated vividly in the run up to the 2003 war in Iraq when a government briefing document examining the Iraqis' threat to external security, produced under high pressure by government officials, was found to have been lifted wholesale from a student's postgraduate thesis.

Similarly, the development of breakthrough technology by the dot.com start-up Napster (see below) enabled it, and similar service providers, to offer Millennials on a tight budget the possibility of downloading music and other entertainment free, thereby bypassing existing copyright restrictions.

Napster's new technology hit the music industry hard. In the spring of 2003 pop star Michael Jackson's finances came under intense scrutiny, prompted by the fact he was being sued by his erstwhile financial advisers, the Union Finance and Investment Corporation of South Korea. Rumours circulated that his excessive lifestyle, costing upwards of $7 million a year, meant that he was running out of money.

Accusations of child abuse in 2004 haven't helped, but the real reason for Jackson's financial problems are equally concerning to the music industry as a whole. His long-term finances were always regarded as secure because at the height of his success he had bought the rights to virtually the complete works of Lennon and McCartney. This should have, on its own, guaranteed him a lifetime pension but the stark fact is that by the first decade of the twenty-first century, the back catalogue of even the most widely bought music does not generate the cash it used to.

The availability of free music, downloaded from the Internet, is punching a great big financial hole in the financial underpinnings of popular music. In 1997 David Bowie had the bright idea of selling off his old songs for £33 million on the stock market. Investors were invited to (literally) buy into Ziggy Stardust, Aladdin Sane and the Thin White Duke.

The future royalties were expected to guarantee excellent returns. Except they didn't. Bowie pocketed the money and the investors took a bath. The reason, once again, was not the declining popularity of Bowie's music but free access to it via the Internet.

Piracy remains the biggest headache facing the record industry. Despite their success in squashing the biggest digital pirate, Napster, in 2002, other online music-swapping services sprung up in its place. File sharing on KaZaA was 1491 per cent higher in June 2002 than in June 2001 according to Comscore Media Metrix, a research group.[6] The industry is suing this and other file-sharing services but new ones emerge as fast as old ones are shut down. Sales of recorded music dropped in 2002 by an estimated 9 per cent. Investing in musicians used to be about building a back catalogue of hits that provide an ongoing source of revenues. But, as the examples of Michael Jackson and David Bowie show, what is the point of a back catalogue if pirates are helping themselves to its tracks for nothing?

Basically the dilemma is this: the products most attractive to Millennials – music, club cocktails, comic books and strips, smart casual clothes, computer games, fantasy films – are the most heavily branded. Brands are incredibly difficult to police and defend, not least in a global market where attitudes to intellectual property rights vary from one country to another. A growing proportion of these products, most notably music but increasingly films, games and comic books and strips, can be easily disseminated over the Net. In the absence of any foolproof means of policing these transactions, the (largely Western) companies who produce these products are reliant on their consumers' willingness to play the game and buy the original.

But, as the crisis faced by Michael Jackson and the thriving trade in bootlegged films and CDs in Thailand and Malaysia illustrate, buying pirated goods is now seen as about as harmless as parking on a yellow line. We found this when interviewing Katya, 20, and her 17-year-old brother Max. Neither had any qualms about buying counterfeit goods.

'At my hairdresser, they had this woman that came in regularly with counterfeit bags to sell that were really good – like you wouldn't know,' says Katya. 'Most people I know have fake ones. You don't see real ones on the street. So, what's the problem? Even if it is real, most people are not going to believe you anyway.'

Max, who is heavily into Nike-branded clothes and shoes, hadn't bought any counterfeit versions but wouldn't have any problem with the idea, provided the quality was OK and the price was right. In any case, he stressed, how can Nike hold its head up high when it has used children in exploitable Asian local communities in order to sell over-priced goods in the West?

Katya and Max also download music on their computers as a matter of course. The determining factor in their decision had little to do with whether it was technically piracy or not but rather the quality of the recorded material and the capacity of their computer's memory.

'I download music all the time,' says Katya. 'The only reason I stopped recently was because I downloaded a virus while doing it. This doesn't mean to say that I never buy CDs. If I found I was downloading songs from artists I like, like Pink or Justin Timberlake, and the first two I down-loaded were good, I'd then buy the CD. You get all the songs on the CD and the quality is better.'

And the fact that this was piracy? 'It's not really piracy,' she retorted. 'They make enough as it is.'

Her brother Max then chipped in: 'My teacher does it, my school friends do it, everybody does it. In any case, older people tape stuff from the radio and video stuff from the television. What's the difference? The only difference is that the quality is better.'

What makes the conversation all the more interesting is that their mother, Carol, is not unsympathetic to their line of argument. Her main objection to either of them buying counterfeit goods is that the quality is likely to be poor, not that the transaction is technically illegal. On the issue of downloading music she was highly supportive.

'You hear so many stories about bands that are being screwed by recording companies that you don't feel you are screwing the bands themselves by downloading their music off the Net. It would be different if the impression was given that you were stopping the band from recording.'

Of course, that is the impression now being given by recording companies. When in June 2003 music companies took their campaign a stage further by threatening to sue not only websites like Napster and Morpheus but also every individual – including children – guilty of using the service, they justified it by claiming that piracy was stifling new, financially vulnerable talent.

Tom (see 'The Provenance of Cool'), whose band Munkster had just returned from gigging at the Greenpeace tent at the UK's Glastonbury Festival when we talked to him, argues precisely the opposite. He argues that Katya and Max's use of websites to test out newly released music is a lifeline to new bands like his own, helping fans discover new artists. 'This is really a rearguard attempt by the big companies to preserve the revenues from their back catalogues. What new bands need more than anything else is to get their material known and out in the market.'

In addition, Katya argues, people in their age range on a student grant or part-time salary share and exchange music rather than hoarding it. 'I and my friends sell second-hand CDs like we do our old textbooks. Amazon are doing a huge trade in this. Are the big music companies going to try to control this too?'

There is also a separate issue of how the ideas and insights that underpin these products are inspired and fostered. New technology has evened the playing field between large and small companies in terms of operational efficiency and service, making the intellectual output of the company its most critical competitive resource. But, as we have already seen in earlier chapters, the individuals most able to invent or reinvent the company's most likely profitable products are the least likely to want to work directly for the organization.

Freedom is the commodity these individuals want to underpin their creative work. Freedom in how they work. Freedom to ask novel or disturbing questions. Freedom to come up with unusual solutions to the things they are thinking about (sometimes in the form of what seems, to others, to be impractical ideas). Yet in a world where ideas are virtually exchanged and the output from these ideas are virtually disseminated, companies are having to resort to increasingly intrusive legal and contractual measures to retain their ownership over this output and the income they gain from it – measures that, inappropriately applied, cut against the very creative grain they are trying to foster.

The attempts by the music industry to clamp down on downloaded music, for example, is skating on thin ice. The decision by the Recording Industry Association of America (RIAA) in June 2003 to target individual consumers with hundreds of lawsuits seeking damages of up to $150,000 for each alleged offence raised legal eyebrows. The clampdown followed an American court ruling that forced Internet service provider Verizon to release the names of four subscribers who the RIAA claimed were illegally trading copyrighted songs. Verizon, believing the decision could lead to a flood of similar lawsuits, has appealed against the decision.

The decision is up in the air in the light of an earlier ruling that Grokster and Morpheus, the two most subscribed to websites after Napster, should not be closed down because they were not deemed to be legally responsible for what is traded on their websites. Fred von Lohmann of the Electronic Frontier Foundation, the leading US lobby group for Internet users, accused the RIAA of attacking its own consumers. 'This latest effort indicates the recording industry has lost touch with reality. Does anyone think more lawsuits are going to be the answer?'[7]

Whatever the immediate outcome of the clampdown, long-term efforts by the music and other industries to use existing legal sanctions to deter a new generation from using technology that is widely available to download free entertainment to an increasingly higher standard seems futile – about as futile as the Catholic Inquisition's attempts to ban Protestant Bibles translated into local languages in the wake of the Caxton printing press.

A far more sensible strategy is to go with the flow generated by hard-nosed Millennials, such as the views expressed by Tom and Katya above, and introduce legal, paid for online services that enable teenagers and young adults to download extracts from upcoming releases at a cheaper price than the CD as a 'try-out'. The legal version of Napster, Napster 2.0, launched in November 2003[8] is likely to profit the industry far more than heavy-handed action taken against their own consumers. It is easy to forget that the original Napster was hailed at the time of its launch by technology pioneers such as Andy Grove as the Hot Idea of the Year that represented 'a different architecture for exchanging information' – and that it was a classic Millennial start-up founded by a 19-year-old and a 20-year-old in a back basement in San Mateo, California.[9]

Nor is the issue about who owns ideas confined to copyright law. In 1995, Japan's leading cosmetics manufacturer Shiseido launched a highly successful skin lotion called Hadasui ('bare skin'). The campaign was notable for the fact that, for the first time in its history, the company based the launch around the originator, a 31-year-old marketing executive called Norika Shimada.

This was a significant break with the faceless traditions of the company, which reflected the mores of Japanese industry as a whole. In the previous two years the company had launched a series of successful products but at no point had they provided any public recognition for the originator.

The role Shimada played in the launch is a testament to the internal struggle she underwent to get the product approved by the board. Hadasui's main ingredient is mineral water from the slopes of Mount Fuji. At the time, there was a boom in sales of mineral water in Japan and Shimada came up with the idea for the product after using mineral water in a number of ways at home.

The marketing concept behind Hadasui – that skin should have mineral water to 'drink' too – did not go down well with Shiseido's conservative senior management. They felt that the message was too 'faddy' and did not fit in well with the company's recent product launches.

Shimada had to lobby individual members of the board intensely, with little or no help from colleagues in her own department. At the same time, she had to leave herself enough time to undertake her day-to-day work. In all, it took nearly a year of lobbying to get the product accepted and a further two years to get it on the market.

Shimada decided to use her own story as the centrepiece for the launch. This too was a departure from tradition. In the event, Japanese newspapers and magazines scrambled to get the story, resulting in major publicity and record sales for the product. 'The launch vindicated my persistence but it was a gamble,' she says. 'If you stick your neck out you have to risk it might get cut off.'[10]

Directors at Shiseido learned many lessons from the Hadasui launch, the most important being that individual recognition is vital in encouraging front-line staff to be more creative. In recent years, they have abolished the internal *sempai-kohai* relationships, where senior managers take precedence in all things, and are addressed by their rank by junior staff.

They have also learned from Shimada's experience that good ideas are often inspired outside the workplace and by making connections with ideas and experiences that are often unrelated to the company's sector or industry. To broaden their experience, senior managers at Shiseido now attend seminars where speakers discuss topics as diverse as international gymnastics and the work of Japan's volunteer medical service in developing countries.

Nor is this merely a matter of discretionary good practice. Two years before the Hadasui launch, Shuji Nakamura of Japan's Nichia Corporation invented blue light-emitting diodes (LEDs). But Mr Nakamura received a paltry sum ($180) for his invention and no extra perks. Rigid local employment practices meant that he was not promoted any faster than colleagues his own age. When he left Nichia in 1999 at the age of 45, he was earning an average salaryman's wage of 16 million yen a year. At international conferences, Western scientists dubbed him 'slave Nakamura'.

When Mr Nakamura sued his former employer for a share of the profits from his invention in 2002, he sent shock waves across corporate Japan. Nichia, he claimed, had made millions of dollars from LEDs, which are now used in traffic lights, household electrical appliances and even medical equipment.[11]

If successful, his lawsuit (which was still working its way through the courts at the time of writing) could cost Nichia as much as 2 billion yen. The law is vague, requiring companies to pay 'adequate compensation' to employees who develop profitable patents. Nichia, like many other companies in Japan, had set (cheap) rates similar to those paid at government-run research institutes. Cocooned in the lifetime-employment system, few employees complained – until recently.

As a consequence, protecting both present and future intellectual assets has become increasingly linked to employee performance. Commercial intelligence suggested to the US company Nortel Networks that it was applying for fewer patents than its principal competitors. The company saw the expansion and protection of its intellectual property rights as a key competitive tool. It was therefore keen to explore ways in which the challenge of developing, filing and successfully gaining patents for key products and technologies could be extended to a broader range of its research and development staff.

Accordingly, Nortel Networks launched a new initiative in 1996, the Intellectual Property Awards and Recognition Plan.

The aim of the plan was threefold:

- To strengthen an environment that was conducive to innovation.
- To encourage all research and scientific staff to become actively involved in developing, filing and securing grants of patents for key products and technologies developed at its research laboratories and development facilities.
- To raise the level of awareness of the importance of intellectual property as a key competitive tool among all staff working for the company.

The plan provides both monetary awards and public recognition for all staff involved in innovation resulting in the filing of patent applications. There are four grades:

- *Patent filing*. This rewards all inventors involved in the preparation of a patent application at the point at which it is filed. The monetary award is paid through the payroll and a framed filing certificate is presented to each inventor at an event at the site where he/she works.
- *Patent issuance*. This rewards inventors who have had a patent successfully issued. The monetary award is paid through the payroll and a laser engraved plaque of the issued patent is presented to each inventor at a specially arranged recognition event.
- *Cumulative awards*. This rewards inventors who have been involved in a number of patent issuances. Awards are made for 5, 10, 15 and so on patent issuances.
- *Significant patent awards*. This rewards inventors who have been involved in the successful issuance of a patent or patents deemed to be of significant value to the company. Examples include patents that have brought in substantial patent licensing revenues, that form the basis of an important industry standard, that protect one of the company's core technologies or products or that have received industry-wide recognition.

For patent issuances, inventors receive a monetary award and a plaque highlighting their achievement. Presentations for these awards are made by a senior Nortel executive in the presence of other patent awardees and have previously taken place at sites of scientific or engineering significance. In the UK, recent patent issuance awards events have taken place at Greenwich Observatory, the Thames Barrier and Bletchley Park, where the German Enigma code was cracked during the World War II.

The awards are highlighted in the company's world-wide electronic newsletters and are sometimes reflected in external media.

In the decade since the plan was launched, there has been a significant increase in the number of invention submissions made by inventors across the company. Not only has the quantity increased but also the quality has improved. More Nortel employees now see themselves as inventors and also view their innovations in a business context, thus increasing the number of successful patent applications.

As Nortel's consultant scientist on its optical communications programme at its Harlow Laboratories stresses, the initiative has not only given new incentive to those of Nortel Networks' research and development staff that were already actively and regularly engaged in patent applications but also the initiative has had a positive effect on the broader Nortel community.

'As a frequent inventor, I get turned on by the creative process itself, and I think the same is true of other regular inventors. The money and the recognition were incidental to the satisfaction we got in breaking new ground. However the Plan has stimulated and intellectually engaged other employees who had not previously considered themselves inventors and given a much needed boost in recognition of the importance of our work within the organization as a whole.'[12]

ISSUE 3

The collapse of the post-World War II social contract means that people in developed countries will have to work well beyond traditional pensionable age to maintain an acceptable standard of living. Changing employment patterns and advances in healthcare may mean that many who do not have to will nonetheless carry on working out of choice. How can organizations seeking to establish a common corporate culture accommodate the needs of workers separated by as many as three generations, whose desire for flexible work may be similar but who have dramatically different values?

Western societies worship youth: but they are also increasingly reliant on the old as both consumers and workers. HR and product development managers are struggling to reconcile the needs of four or more generations in a similar marketplace – and the difficulties are immense.

The most obvious example is in branding. Companies that have used high branded products to target teenagers and people in their early 20s have long since realized that there is no way they can make the 'brand' (as opposed to the clothes, drinks, foods etc. they are promoting) appeal simultaneously to more than one generation.

The war for talent has banished a lot of rules. Once they go away, they tend not to come back.
Robert Morgan,
US head-hunter, Spherion

In his book *Brandchild*,[13] which charts the relationship of children to brands, author Martin Lindstrom takes the same view as *Newsweek* journalist Thomas Lank (see 'Outside Cool'). If you are to appeal to a group that is inherently anti-establishment, the brand has to be 'anti'. 'The cool ones are the anti-brands,' says Lindstrom, who predicts that underneath a global umbrella brand, companies will divide their lines into hundreds or even thousands of individual brands.

Easier said than done. Levi's found to its cost in the late 1990s that a brand image painstakingly built up among baby boomers over the previous three decades was not so easily transferable to Millennials, who deserted the brand in droves in favour of rivals Hilfiger. Hilfiger's logos and iconography, deliberately based on urban rappers, teen film stars and Web-surfers, appealed to Millennials' own values (see

'Outside Cool'). Levi's was forced to follow suit. Fast food giant McDonald's recently attempted to water down a three-decade-old brand aimed at children and teenagers, using the Ronald McDonald clown, by developing derivative products and ads aimed at professional adult workers. But initiatives such as the 'Things That Make You Go Mmm' campaign, designed to broaden its appeal across the board, did not prevent, and arguably contributed to, its first annual losses in 2003.

A similar issue faces HR practitioners attempting to reconcile different workplace needs. The two groups at the opposite end of the generational scale, under 25s and the over 50s, share common ground – neither are tied to time-consuming parental responsibilities. This means that, despite their different expectations, employers are resorting to the same means to recruit and retain both of them.

In the late 1990s, for example, IBM in Belgium – faced with the need to cut staff costs and having decided to concentrate cuts on 55–60-year-olds – set up a separate company called SkillTeam, which re-employed any of the early retired who wanted to go on working up to the age of 60.[14] An employee who joined SkillTeam at the age of 55 on a five-year contract would work for 58 per cent of his time, over the full period, for 88 per cent of his last IBM salary. The company offered services to IBM, thus allowing it to retain access to some of the intellectual capital it would otherwise have lost.

The best way to tempt the old to go on working may be to build on such 'bridge' jobs: part-time or temporary employment that creates a more gradual transition from full-time work to retirement. Joseph Quinn, an economist at Boston College, who has studied the growing moves of US firms to retain the skills of their retiring workers, found that as many as half of all men and women who had previously been in full-time jobs in middle age moved into such 'bridge' jobs at the end of their working lives.

In general, he stresses, it is the best paid and worst paid that carry on working. 'There are two very different types of bridge job-holders – those who continue working because they have to and those who continue working because they want to, even though they could afford to retire.' And among those who have a choice it will, as he puts it, 'have to be more fun than touring around in an Airstream trailer, or seeing the grandchildren, or playing golf.'[15]

The similarities these types of older worker share with Millennials are striking. Both groups are attracted to flexible patterns of work because it tops up other sources of income: grants, pensions, revenue from their own self-employed activities. Both have reduced needs for fixed incomes. Both have other 'worlds' and other agendas and part-time or temporary work form only one facet of a larger lifestyle agenda. But the values of each are radically different, as is the language they use and their attitudes to proprietorial working space, the use of technology as a relationship-builder from scratch and the time of day they are most willing to give up to paid employment.

British Airways found this when they moved 2500 of their administrative staff into a purpose-built headquarters in 1997. The move to the new building was accompanied by working practices designed to encourage an office-less culture. Under what the designers termed 'club working', employees did not have a desk of their own and kept their work equipment in large filing drawers. They then chose a working space designed for the particular kind of work they wanted to engage in at the time.

There were workspaces designed for private reflection and study, for collective team discussions, for individual computer work and for greeting and entertaining guests. A new communications system enabled one to 'touchdown' from anywhere inside or outside the building, checking up on new appointments and messages. Everyone was encouraged to conduct business in a corporate boulevard with its own shops, cafes and restaurants in order to stimulate cross-departmental serendipity. The boulevard was the only means of walking from one workspace to another, so staff from different departments inevitably 'bumped into each other' in a way that did not happen in the old administrative buildings.

The trouble was, BA tested out the new methods of working with the staff most likely to welcome it rather then those who were likely to find the break with the past most threatening. The pilot scheme tried out club working on the relationship marketing department, made up of young, technically proficient professionals who were naturally peripatetic in their day-to-day work and most open to new ideas.

Once the move had taken place, BA found that older administrators in the legal and financial departments objected to not having their 'own' workspace. Senior managers' personal assistants also disliked the no-office culture because it meant that their role as the 'gatekeepers and guardians' of their boss's itinerary and work schedule was undermined.

Almost immediately, the company was forced to backtrack, allowing administrative departments the right to revert back to older working methods. The whole project had been championed by the outgoing chief executive Bob Ayling and once his successor Rod Eddington took over, many of the fancier workspace design concepts were ditched – not least the idea that board-level directors and the chief executive did not need their own offices.

BA's difficulties in reconciling the needs of different generations of workers reflects a broader social gulf. In his research on how people relate to time (outlined in more detail in 'Outside Cool'), Michael Willmott of the Future Foundation found a stark contrast between 'fast-laners' (under 30s without children who form 25 per cent of all adults) and 'past timers' (over 60s whose children have left home who form 27 per cent of all adults).[16]

While fast-laners tend to feel fairly time pressured, they do not think that the pace of life is too fast and they believe that their lives would be enhanced if services were available 24 hours a day. Their view of the 24-hour society is hedonistic and bound up with the immediate satisfaction of their wants. By contrast, 'past-timers' do not feel time pressured – but believe, nonetheless, that the world is now moving too fast. They see no need for 24-hour services. Rather, they would like the world to slow down and be like it was in the past.

Language and humour is another example. In 1997 Andy Allan, director of programmes at the UK independent television station Carlton, sparked off a furious debate between comedy writers when he told a seminar at the Golden Rose Festival in Montreux that television humour was failing older people. Executives, he argued, were too ready to cave in to advertisers, who want to appeal to 16- to 35-year-olds. 'Our comedy producers have got to the stage where they feel it is almost immoral to make anyone over fifty laugh.'

In the subsequent furore, John Sullivan, writer of timeless mainstream UK comedy classics such as *Only Fools and Horses* and *Citizen Smith* added, 'One thing we seem to be doing wrong is using bad language. I'm not in the least sensitive to Anglo-Saxon words but so many writers seem to use a naughty word when they can't think of anything funny to say. I call it "shag humour" and it seems to have come from university and the alternative comedy circuit. If you don't know how to finish a scene on a laugh, just get a character to end a speech with the word shag. It's lazy writing.'[17]

Use of bad language regularly tops the pole in both North America and the United Kingdom as the biggest source of complaints from broadcast viewers or listeners. A ban on bad language is rigorously enforced on mainstream US broadcasts, less so (particularly after a 9 p.m. threshold) in the UK. Yet, as we have already seen, the use of swear words is an integral part of the films, video games, comedy club circuit patters and broadcasts specifically aimed at Millennials – and attempts to ban it on company intranets represents one of the many 'controlling' aspects of corporate communications that the under-25s find oppressive.

SUMMARY AND CONCLUSIONS

In summary, the great challenge over the next two decades will be to create management and employment practices that cut across as many as four generations working simultaneously for the organization. Ron Zempke, Claire Raines and Bob Filipczak, authors of *Generations at Work: Managing the Clash of Boomers, Xers and Nexters in Your Workplace* came up in 2000 with a five-point strategy:[18]

1   *Accommodate employee differences*. Learn about employees as you would about your customers. Make real efforts to accommodate personal needs.
2   *Create workplace choices*. Shape the workplace around the tasks being accomplished, the customers' needs, and the employees.

3   *Operate from a sophisticated management style.* Monitor and alter supervisory styles based on the individual employee. Create a situationally varied leadership style where some decisions are made by the manager (with input) and others are consensus-driven. (See also guidelines in 'Managing Cool'.)

4   *Respect competence and initiative.* Hire carefully and assume the best in your people, young and old.

5   *Nourish retention.* Make your workplace a magnet for excellence by encouraging lateral movement, with broad job assignments. Offer lots of training (from mentoring through computer-based to classroom – see 'Inside Cool'), and continue to market internally to your employees.

PART TWO

PART TWO

COOL LEADERSHIP

6

Professor Garth Saloner, head of Stanford University's e-business and commerce department and a veteran observer of Silicon Valley management, remarked recently that while he would happily entrust 'Nintendo Kids' (aka Millennials) to go out and create something cool with some discretionary venture capital, he would not in a million years entrust them with the management of a serious enterprise.

'They have speed but haven't got a clue what they are doing,' he says. 'A 50 or 60-year-old manager can make decisions in a nanosecond too because they are experienced. The difference is that they will be good decisions.'[1]

Amid all the talk about 'reverse mentoring' and surrounding yourself with 'cyber frenzy', the cautionary talk after the excesses of the dot.com boom and crash is that the energy and speed of Generation X and Millennial-era professionals need to be tempered with good old-fashioned experience – someone who, as Saloner puts it, 'knows how to do a deal and how to manage.'

However, dot.com enterprises are not the only – and certainly not the first – instance in which kids barely off the block have either founded their own business or been promoted into senior corporate jobs. Since running your own enterprise became sexy again in the early 80s, at least in the United States and Britain, a steady stream of teenage or twentysomething executives, trading on their 'cool' approach to business, have hit the headlines.

Many of the most successful, as this chapter will show, are second- or third-generation siblings from Asian or Middle Eastern immigrant families who have combined their knowledge of popular trends and fashions in their new home country, and how these translate into durable brands, with the entrepreneurial energy and dynamism of their diaspora-based families. Where they have succeeded, it is because – taking into account Professor's Saloner's reservations – they have recognized their limitations as well as their strengths.

AJAZ AHMED: DIGITALLY TUNED INTO BRANDS

Celebrities like Madonna and Tiger Woods and football clubs like Manchester United and Arsenal have this much in common: they constantly reinvent themselves to stay relevant.

Ajaz Ahmed, just turned 30, is typical of this breed. He founded one of the UK's most successful digital communications agencies, AKQA, when he was just 22. It's a £50 million a year business now. He had no track record in business management prior to then, having worked for the 1980s software leader Ashton-Tate as a dogsbody and in a variety of relatively junior product development jobs at Apple Computer.

But he had an instinctive grasp of how the various strands of communications came together in the digital age. Matthew Treagus, managing director of AKQA's Washington DC and Dallas operations, commented in 2002: 'Ajaz has an instinctive understanding of brands, consumers, technology and business, and his ability to reconcile these discrete disciplines without compromise has been the key to AKQA's success.'

Within six years of founding the business, however, Ahmed handed over the day-to-day running of the business to a professional manager, Tom Bedecarre, in order to concentrate of what he is best at: forging new alliances and managing strategic accounts. Now AKQA's global chairman, he had no qualms about handing over the reins.

Free from the bureaucracy of managing a global corporation, he can ensure that the factor that distinguishes AKQA from the also-rans – its ability to help corporate clients see their products and services from a customer's point of view, and then plan and develop ways for clients to interact with their customers across multiple platforms including the Internet, call centres, mobile devices and digital TV – is not watered down or compromised.

He was the personal mastermind behind Nike's immensely successful 'Run London' event in 2001. The aim was to persuade London's commuters to sign up to the event as active participants. Nike ran an integrated publicity campaign but the online work – created by AKQA – continued afterwards. The 10,000 places were filled within a week of the website going live, and it also allowed people to send text messages and movies to friends to encourage them to run. After the event, people could even type in their finish time and view a video of themselves crossing the finish line.

Ahmed recognized early the two most important principals of staying alive in a modern communications industry: interact and reinvent – constantly. AKQA was the first agency to treat a company website not just as an online brochure but also as a medium for the entire business cycle, from initial interest to purchase. In 2002, the agency formed an alliance with Treatment, a company that builds brands through TV and films.

'Companies can build their brands more quickly and have more impact through associations with a film or TV series,' Ahmed explained in a recent interview.[2] 'The media landscape is changing as the number of channels proliferate. Innovative companies have an unprecedented opportunity to shift consumer behaviour and create trends rather than just following them. In a marketplace crowded with brands, those that create a new trend will stand out.'

BOBBY AND SAHAR HASHEMI: A SKINNY LATTE IN THE MAKING

We all have the image of the typical swashbuckling entrepreneur who drops out of school having made millions selling worms in kindergarten or sweets in the playground. [But] If you are someone ordinary, it is a bit daunting.

Sahar Hashemi started the entrepreneurial game young – in her mid-20s – but from a respectable legal career. Her brother, two years older, had a career in corporate finance behind him. The enterprise they set up – a UK version of the coffee bars they had enjoyed slipping into during business trips to New York called Coffee Republic – has enjoyed dramatic, possibly meteoric, success. The first branch opened in London's South Molton Street in 1995. Angel investment of £600,000 allowed the siblings to open six more stores the following year. In 1997 the venture went public and in the following four years 90 outlets were set up around the country.

It sounds simple, but it wasn't. It was Bobby's ambition to become an entrepreneur, not Sahar's. She took time off to write the business plan, which identified the cardinal importance of a distinct brand. But she had never had any idea other than to be a lawyer and was reluctant to chuck it in. Any rose-tinted view about being in business for themselves was quickly dispelled for both of them once they set about it. Nineteen banks rejected their proposal and they had to obtain the support of the Small Firm Loan Guarantee Scheme to raise the cash.

The plan required the first outlet to make an average of £700 a day in the first six months to break even. They made £200. The press took no notice. In the US the Seattle Coffee Company had opened at the same time and the possibility of a growth race haunted them. Eventually Bobby's ex-boss offered him his old job back.

Once the constraints of the initial start-up period were vaulted, the pair faced the inevitable implications of growth. Sahar, for all her initial shyness of business, had proved the entrepreneurial force behind the enterprise. But, unlike Anita Roddick, she had no illusions that the force of her personality was going to reach the outer orbits of a company that had 90 stores in city centres around the UK. As a consequence, Coffee Republic hired the branded sandwich outlet Prêt-à-Manger's operations director Rod McKie to manage the operations while she struggled to keep the soul of the enterprise alive as the brand and marketing director.

This was no easy job. By the turn of the decade, the market had become saturated with brands that were not sufficiently distinguishable. Compared with the three main others – Starbucks, Costa Coffee and Caffe Nero – Coffee Republic was easily the weakest. Sahar and Bobby both left the board in April 2001. At the time of writing, Bobby had returned to the company as executive chairman and Sahar was trading on her experience, with the launch of a how-to book, *Anyone Can Do It*. The company was the subject of a possible takeover bid from Caffe Nero and under pressure to sell several of its sites to Starbucks.

SHAMI AHMED: NOT YER ORDINARY JOE BLOGGS

People do not know what I am looking for. The agenda changes in my head all the time.

If G.K. Noon ('Inside Cool') is representative of the first generation of Britain's new breed of Asian entrepreneurs, Shami Ahmed personifies the values of the next. A born and bred Brit in his own eyes, he has pioneered the brash UK fashion style that has made its mark in Europe precisely because it owes little to continental traditions. The Legendary Joe Bloggs, the company he founded in 1985 when he was 24, is now one of the UK's leading manufacturers of jeans, denim jackets, T-shirts and sweatpants.

Now in his 40s, Shami left school at the age of 16 to work with his father in the family's Manchester-based fashion wholesale business, Pennywise. The eight years he worked there was enough for him to get an acute eye for unexplored gaps. In the 1980s, young people in the north of England had more disposable income than many retailers realized. Designer jeans, however, were out of their financial reach. Like Noon, Shami exploited new technology that enabled him to offer jeans with a wide range of washes, enabling a mass market product to be individualized at a price young people could afford.

At the turn of the century, Joe Bloggs had achieved a brand awareness of around 85 per cent and was one of the top-selling jeans in Britain. At the time of writing, after a decade managing Joe Bloggs himself, Shami was preparing to enter a new phase in the company's history by recruiting a senior management team that could take over the task, releasing him to plan further diversification and to pursue private interests.

Shami Ahmed's best business idea, inventing the Joe Bloggs brand, says a lot about the formative influences that inspired him. 'I wanted something unmistakably British,' he says, 'something that personified where I came from and who I was. At the same time, it had to be a brand that I could market around the world. As for adding the word 'Legendary', I knew the enterprise was going to be big and I decided that instead of waiting until someone else created an epithet after the event, I would create my own. Everybody laughed when I tried out the name and that was precisely the reaction I wanted.'[3]

The first factor is Shami's British roots. His early target market was British, particularly from the north. The appeal to an international market is the down-to-earth yet stylish feel that has marked out new British products in the 1990s and he has financed his business using British banks and financial institutions, unlike many older Asian entrepreneurs who have looked to their own community for finance and support.

The influence of his father, who brought him into the fashion industry, has therefore been mixed. 'My father gave me integrity and the sense that it is always better to create your own success, rather than taking it from someone else. He also instilled in me the importance of looking after the family. I have a strong sense of working for the next generation. Yet things move on. First-generation Asians kept everything close to their chests. In my world, people need to know what you are doing. Market demand is led by what you are as well as what you offer. That is part of the brand. The difference between my parents' style of business and my own amounts to that.'

The second factor is therefore Shami's outgoing management style. Breaking with the low-key and introspective traditions of his father's generation, he boasts an elite clientele of pop stars and actively markets his company through high-profile associations with pop groups. In 1994, he accepted a commission to produce the most expensive pair of jeans in the world for the pop star Prince, worth more than £100,000.

The internal culture and business methods of Joe Bloggs are equally upfront. Shami encourages young, enthusiastic and streetwise people to work for him. A sophisticated in-house export department manages overseas accounts and works closely with the marketing team to ensure that monthly bulletins on Joe Bloggs's activities are forwarded to all distributors worldwide.

Shami's success is founded on having a close knowledge of the emerging tastes of a market made up predominately of under-25s. His thirst for information, any information that keeps him in touch with changing trends, informs what and how he reads.

In contrast with most senior managers, who are highly focused in their reading, Shami reads 'anything and everything' that is close to his market. In addition to virtually all the daily and weekend papers, tabloid and quality, he pores over women's magazines, trade periodicals, teenage fanzines and the new range of men's magazines such as *GQ* and *Arena*. Whenever he has a long train or plane journey, he buys armfuls of publications from the newsagent.

The sheer volume of newsprint he purchases means that he can do little more than skim through the headings and intros but it is enough to provoke a steady stream of new insights and ideas. 'Everybody asks why I do not use a cuttings service, or set one up myself,' he says. 'I tried, but it didn't work. The people do not know what you are looking for, even if they work for you. The agenda in my head changes all the time. If there has been a change in the share price of a company, for example, I might be more interested in reading an article about them one day than I was the previous week.'[4]

This acquisition of market information extends, albeit less systematically, into his leisure activities. He still sees a movie at weekends and although his primary purpose is to relax, his tastes – popular Hollywood blockbusters – are also those of his market. 'In a way it is like reading a magazine,' he says. 'You see the changing trends in what people are wearing, eating and listening to, and it all gets processed. It is surprising how often this kind of casually acquired information helps me make a decision a few weeks later.'

Catholic in what he reads or watches, Shami is more focused in his networking. He does not attend or speak at conferences and he confines formal networking outside the fashion industry to a monthly meeting of the Young Presidents Association, a worldwide forum of young chief executives who take it in turn to host meetings.

Shami has high praise for the YPA. 'It is a bit like having a team of non-executive directors giving you impartial advice,' he says. However he is more sceptical about traditional networking. 'There are too many people out there wanting too many favours. There is a tendency for people to abuse the system.'

This does not mean that he is blind to what he can learn from the business world. Although he does not engage in formal benchmarking, he is a great student of other people's businesses, skimming through the business pages of the newspapers and taking advantage of any access his position gives him in acquiring an inside view of a company that has caught his eye.

'I am always gathering knowledge,' he says. 'You can learn from what other businesses do right and what they do wrong. It helps to balance any decision you make, even if you are not completely sure.'

RICARDO SEMLER: QUESTIONING LIKE A CHILD

We believe in the virtues of dissent. We don't want a crowd of workers singing the company song. We listen, and if the dissenter is right, maybe we can all learn something.

You wouldn't think it when you see fortysomething Ricardo Semler at the head of his $100 million turnover engineering and consultancy business Semco, but his biggest interest when he joined the firm was to play in a rock and roll band. The first thing that comes into your head is that you could not find two activities further apart; yet the inspiration for many of the reforms Semler has made to the business since he inherited from his father at the age of 21 came from his days as a musician.

In an age when the 'value added' of firms lies in the knowledge and creativity of its workers, Semler saw giving people a reason to come into work as a most important task when he took over. Just as the drummer in his band could not be persuaded to turn up at rehearsal if he did not feel motivated, so he reasoned that staff at Semco would only really contribute to the company on a grey Monday morning if the atmosphere in which they work kept them feeling excited.

Bit by bit, Semler dismantled the company's very conservative culture. At first, this consisted of eliminating patently outdated practices such as searching employees as they left at the end of the day and the use of time clocks. But this was followed by measures that are seen as radical even by today's standards, including the removal of all controls over working hours and working dress and new rules governing pay which now mean that one-third of employees set their own salaries while the rest are negotiated within business units according to performance.

Some of his ideas in the first years were even more wacky. One example was a board with three pegs by each employee's name for them to hang a coloured flag on each morning: green for 'good mood', yellow for 'careful' and red for 'not today, thank you'. Staff took to it immediately. However, a later trial of 'mobile offices' – desk on wheels, 'parked' at the end of the day – was less successful.

Semler's business philosophy was not a commercial form of anarchy. His kind of freedom came laden with responsibilities. Managers were elected by their subordinates and evaluated by them every six months. Those that didn't come up to scratch could be moved sideways, downwards or out. Business units set their own targets but once they set them, they had to meet them.

Not surprisingly, such a radical approach was difficult to sell to the company's traditional stakeholders. A number of senior managers left and Semler spent two or three years 'running from bank to bank just to get enough capital to keep going for another month or two'. But since the mid-1980s, growth has been almost linear. Turnover rose from $35 million to $100 million in the first five years of the last decade. In the seven years that followed it increased sevenfold, despite the fact that Semler lost some of his own money in a dot.com venture that when belly-up in the 2001 crash.

Now, far from being dismissed as latter-day Trotskyite, Semler is lauded for his reforms. His basic tenet – that people and companies perform best when left to themselves

– has inspired similar reforms among a number of manu-facturing companies in the US, schools in Finland, an Aus-tralian hospital and the Amsterdam police force.

'When employees are given control [over the way they work] they act in their own interest, which will be in the in-terest of the business,' he commented in a recent interview. 'We believe in the virtues of dissent. We don't want a crowd of workers singing the company song. We listen, and if the dissenter is right, maybe we can all learn something.'[5]

Central to this philosophy is total transparency in what the company makes and what everybody earns. It is Sem-ler's proud boast that the cleaner in his office can look up not only what his salary is but also what his last business trip cost. 'All our company's finance details are available to staff,' he says. 'Those who can't read profit and loss sheets are trained to do so.'

Semler is also an advocate of the idea that innovative managers maintain a broad range of personal and pro-fessional interests (see 'Inside Cool'). He writes business books. The first, *Maverick*, was published in 1995. The fol-low up, *The Seven Day Weekend*, was published in 2003. But his 'extracurricular activities' are far wider. In addition to indulging his interest in rock and roll he has ambitions to become a playwright. His first play, *Checkmates*, opened in Sao Paulo in Brazil, where his company is based, in 1998. Another is on the cards.

COMMON GROUND

All the individuals in this chapter ran their own show young. With the exception of the Hashemi brother and sister part-nership, none of them had any experience of corporate or professional work. None had management experience.

This wasn't a handicap. All of them had the sense to realize their limitations and buy in the services of experienced executives to run the operational end, leaving them to do what they knew best – tapping their insight into the market. All of them grew up in a media revolution in which perception dominates reality. The consequence – that in a sophisticated or mature market people buy a product or a service because they believe in what it stands for and not just because it does the job – was overlooked by executives twice their age with three times their experience.

Establishing brand value and exploiting brand equity underpinned the launch and sustaining strategy of AKQA, Joe Bloggs, and Coffee Republic. The irreplaceable contribution Ajaz Ahmed, Shami Ahmed and Sahar Hashemi brought to their businesses was their ability to tap the aspirations and values of their generation in order to create the identity behind the brand.

In this sense, Generation X and Y entrepreneurs draw their lead from the daddy of them all, Richard Branson. Branson's enterprise took off after a very slow start because he recognized that, while he excelled at providing the drive and courage to break in and shake up previously complacent industries, he lacked the skills to manage the follow-through. He coined the name Virgin in recognition of his then non-existent management abilities. 'My skills are finding the right people to run companies and coming up with new ventures,' he stressed in the 1970s.[6]

His real break came in 1981 when he recruited Robert Devereux, then a 25-year-old at publishers Macmillan, to grow the company's infant communications activities. The territories Devereux explored, mainly in film and video distribution, wound up accounting for three-quarters of the communications division's £43 million turnover by 1987. In a similar way, free rein was given to Simon Draper, music's chairman, who built and developed Virgin's record labels for nearly two decades. Branson, by the way, is tone deaf.

He constantly looked for ways to bring diversity and stretch into the Group's portfolio of businesses. A protracted takeover of W.H. Allen in 1987 gave him the marketing and distribution network he needed to build a sizeable UK publishing house; while a minority stake in Mastetronic, a market leader in computer games, gave him an entrée into electronic publishing. In the same year, Virgin had become a founder shareholder of British Satellite Broadcasting (BSB), the company had just opened its first sweetshop and Branson was exploring record deals to broaden the music division's portfolio into classical jazz, Third World and children's records.

In the wake of the company's mixed success in focusing on train and air travel in the 1990s, and the publicity cliché he himself became, it is easy to forget how eclectic Branson was at this point and the extent to which he anticipated corporate brand management advances in the following decade. 'I like getting my teeth into new challenges,' he said in an interview for a magazine in 1986. 'I like making things work when others are sceptical and surprising the pundits.'

It is also worth stressing that where an entrepreneur's insight into his or her management limitations is lacking, and no experienced manager is available to provide the backroom underpinning, no multitude of fingers on the pulse of the market will save the business.

Boo.com led the pack of aspiring dot.com businesses prior to the 2001 crash. In 1999, it was one of the most talked about of the UK's start-ups. With offices in Carnaby Street, a mission to sell sportswear and 28-year-old ex-model Kajsa Leander as one of its three founders, all of whom were under 30, it attracted unheard of finance for a venture with little proven capability – something in the order of £74 million from the likes of the Bennetton family, JP Morgan, Sedco and Bain Capital.

A year later, after a launch dogged by technical problems due to the sophistication of its on-site software, the venture was haemorrhaging money. Punters did not come flocking and when they did, they could not get into the website. A 40 per cent across the board sale along with a wave of redundancies failed to turn around the losses. In the wake of the 2001 crash it was bought up by a 'sensible' American company,[7] which revamped the strategy, advising people what to buy rather than selling it to them.

Similarly, few aspiring business entrepreneurs had their fingers more closely clamped on the pulse of youth entertainment than 'ginger-nut' disk jockey Chris Evans. In the wake of his spectacular bust-up with Virgin Radio, a station he once owned – amid drink binging, a period in self-imposed exile and a subsequent law case for wrongful dismissal, which he lost – many commentators have lost sight of just how powerful a business force he was in the late 1990s.

His purchase of Virgin from under the nose of his personally appointed rival Capital Radio in 1997 was the zenith of an extraordinary career as a minor media mogul who had barely turned 30. Branson had wanted to sell the radio station to Capital in a deal worth £87 million that would have given him a ten per cent share in the new holding group. Evans did not want to work for Capital, which he described as a 'bleating, blowing asthmatic dog'.

With the backing of a £42.5 million loan from Banque Paribas and £24 million from Apax, he paid Branson two million less than the Capital offer by offering him a 20 per cent stake in the new company and appealing to his 'maverick' conscience. A year after the Virgin coup, the operating profits of his Ginger Media group were up 72 per cent to £10.5 million, from £6.1 million the previous year. Combined turnover was up 29 per cent to £40.4 million from £32.1 million.

Evans can top even Richard Branson as a role model for all putative child entrepreneurs – all the more because, unlike Branson, he came from a decidedly unprivileged working class background, spending most of his childhood on a Warrington council estate. Evans ran a squad of newspaper boys at a local newsagent's and operated an unofficial sweetshop at his school. 'Running a company has been in my mind for years,' he said when closing the Virgin deal. 'I believe absolutely in one man having the vision for the way something should be done.'

For the latter half of the decade, Evans was the biggest thing to hit UK broadcasting – in cultural and business terms. From a humble start as a bit player on Piccadilly Radio to his Radio 1 breakfast programme and through to his Channel 4 hit series *TFI Friday* and ultimately Virgin Radio, he invariably had his finger on the pulse. His ability to pull the rug from under Capital was based on the fact that he was *the* star turn at Virgin, raising the breakfast listening audience from 1.8 million to 2.6 million within three months of joining the station.

Evans is no fool. When he wants to, he can really impress. Barbara Manfrey of Apax, explaining why the company had backed Evans in the Virgin deal, told the *Daily Telegraph*: 'You have to separate his business persona from his TV and radio persona. He has encyclopedic knowledge of radio and TV and an understanding of it in terms of the market. [When negotiations began] I was very impressed with him. He had a good understanding of what he wanted to do and he articulated it very clearly.'[8]

Unfortunately for his, and Manfrey's, reputation, Evans himself seemed increasingly incapable of separating his two personas. In retrospect, it was harbinger of the future when he quit Radio 1 because its controller Matthew Bannister refused to allow him Fridays off. Soon afterwards, he described himself as medically unsound on his Channel 4 *TFI* set, while brandishing containers of prescription drugs, amid officially sanctioned talk of nervous exhaustion.

The demons returned five years later when Evans took unofficial sick leave from Virgin and was then seen in alcoholic binges at his local pub with his new wife, pop star Billie Piper. Whether his gratuitous self-destruction was prompted by fatal flaws in his personality caused by the death of his father from cancer when he was 14 (as had been exhaustively trawled over by the media psychologists), a serious case of alcoholism, the knowledge that his ratings were falling and that he had lost his winner instinct, sheer boredom – or a combination of all these – Evans was burned out by the time he exited Virgin.

His business strategy – whether it was buying Virgin, negotiating with Talk Radio to bid for digital radio licences or, as seemed at one point possible, attempting to take over the *Star* from the Express Group – was based on the principle equity of any deal being his own talent and reputation. By the time of the Virgin bust-up, he had stopped reinventing himself. He once commented that once his father had died, there was nothing else to be scared of in life, but he admitted afterwards that he was always fearful of losing control. This demon continued to dog him throughout his career – and still does.

SUMMARY

In this sense, Stanford's Silicon Valley expert Professor Saloner's comment that he would never in a million years let a Nintendo Kid run a major business is missing the point.

If the Nintendos have any common sense, they wouldn't either. Most successful entrepreneurs over the last two decades know their limitations. They leave running the business to the people who know how.

Yet leaving the mechanics to experienced professionals doesn't mean that the 'out of the box' thinking that Millennials offer when they come to a new business has no place. The one exception to the group above, Ricardo Semler, illustrates this in spades. Like all the others, he came to business a virgin. Unlike the others, he focused on operations rather than purely on strategy and his very naivety was his main contribution. 'I like to ask the question "why" more than a small child and I do it for the same reasons. There isn't a single reform I have implemented that hasn't been questioned by senior management. When appalled executives ask me why I think, say, introducing catnapping at work will not work, I ask why it won't. They usually do not get past three "why" questions.'[9]

Nor is he alone. Michael Furdyk and Michael Hayman closely followed Semler's example in the company they co-founded in March 1999, Buybuddy.com, an online computer and software comparison shopping service. Furdyk was 16 at the time and Hayman 19. Most of their staff were in their late teens and early 20s. A hallmark of the company was an open space work environment where employees were free to shape the work environment to their own tastes with sofas, pillows and throw rugs as the most popular and inexpensive furnishings.

Microsoft, from its inception right up to its current status at the top of its industry with 40,000 mostly young-ish staff, adopted an anything goes culture. The only dress code is 'bathe'. Extreme body piercing, shorts and blue hair are commonplace, even in some managers. The only things the company bans outright are guns and smoking. Richard

Branson has always been keen on promoting insiders, and took a lead in encouraging company loyalty with incentive and share option schemes. Stability among top executives and staff loyalty were hallmarks of the company during this period.

Key points

- Successful entrepreneurs who start their businesses young are closer to the market and more capable of creating a brand with an identity that will appeal to the latest market. That is what they bring to the business. They are generally not natural born managers and usually sensible enough to recognize it.
- The determining factor is not the launch or the early start-up but the roll out. To succeed, the entrepreneur brings in an experienced professional to tackle the implications of the growth. But the roles are different and not to be confused. The role of the executive is to consolidate the business. The role of the entrepreneur is to keep looking for new markets and keep the brand fresh.
- Nonetheless, naivety is no bad thing in organizational terms if it uses simple 'why' questions to confront entrenched thinking and outdated practices.

MANAGING COOL

The quality of management in most companies – meaning their ability to make you want to get up in the morning raring to get to work – is piss poor. I have a boss at the moment that I want to work hard for. But it's down to him, not the company. If he were to be replaced by someone more typical, I would rather stay at home or help my boyfriend run his business.

Sam (see 'The Provenance of Cool')

One of the most important conclusions we reached from our interviews is that loyalty, when it is given, is a purely local affair. Millennials tend to be as suspicious of 'corporate' branding as they are of product branding. Starting from the assumption that they do not have a long-term future with the company, Millennials take the view that what you see – in terms of the people they work for – is what you get.

This puts a premium on the leadership qualities demonstrated by front-line managers and supervisors. Already responsible for determining whether their work units stay well-motivated in productive terms, local managers are also increasingly the determining factor in whether their organizations attract and keep the right staff.

What competencies and capabilities are involved?

CREATIVE CHALLENGING

What they [new students] are saying to us is, 'Tell me something that I didn't know I needed to know. Challenge me. Astonish me.'
  Caroline Buller, Cranfield School of Management

Characteristic

Millennials like to be intellectually engaged. They are attracted to work that provides them with skills, insights and experiences that they can use in their broader career or 'life' agendas.

Opportunity

They are always open to a new idea or challenge provided they themselves 'own' it.

Threat

They have low boredom thresholds and little staying power unless the energy and personal relevance of the task or goal is constantly sustained.

Response

Managers should be willing to champion, shape and foster new ideas (see Table 7.1). This is not always the case. Our research on innovation for the Roffey Park Institute – based on in-company research with organizations as diverse as

Table 7.1 Five key roles in ideas development

Role	Definition	Often undertaken by
Spark	The person who 'sparks' the creative process by spotting or coming up with the idea, creating the vision or defining the need	Anyone employed by or associated with the organization. Often comes from the least expected area
Sponsors	The people who promote the idea or project inside the organization, ensuring that it is not dismissed and who sustain interest during difficult or lean times	Senior line managers, members of the board, non-executive directors
Shapers	The people who make the idea or project 'real', using their own creativity to flesh out the premise and/or find practical means to achieve the objective	Members of the project team appointed to implement the idea, process-oriented consultants, R&D staff from key suppliers
Sounding boards	People outside the project whose objectivity and broader knowledge can be drawn on to inform and validate the premise or to comment on the practicalities	Informal or formal members of personal or professional networks, trusted colleagues or company-appointed mentors, strategy-oriented consultants, academics or researchers in the field
Specialists	People who draw on their specialist skills to shape the idea or project from a specific standpoint and use the opportunity to break new ground in the field	Members of the project team, consultants (process and strategy), academics and researchers, R&D staff from key suppliers

Source: Roffey Park Institute, 2000

British Airways, Save the Children and the Royal National Orthopaedic Hospital – suggests that a lack of original thinking by front-line staff was not seen as the main problem.[1] Rather it was that not enough of the ideas on the ground were picked up and properly exploited. Exchanges of ideas and insights between individuals – and the joint development of these ideas by groups as a whole – should be an integral part of effective teamwork. Team leaders should not feel that they are 'paid to know it all' but 'paid to uncover it all'.

Example

Anthony Jay, the former BBC producer of hit programmes such as *Yes, Minister* and founder of the cutting-edge video training company Video Arts, once described the output of creative groups in this way:

> *Output is necessary in the first instance as a spur to ideas: the knowledge that a deadline is approaching, that something has to be done urgently, is a wonderful liberator of the creative impulse. That is why the 'wastage' principle does not work with creative groups. The idea of getting ten groups all to put in an idea from which one will be selected and nine discarded does not get the best out of these groups: the sense of urgency is divided by ten. It is much better, very often, for the one group to bear the responsibility alone, to know that everything depends on what they are coming up with, and that good or bad it will go into production because there is nothing else.[2]*

CONTINUOUS COACHING

> *There is always something new to experience and to learn from. I like the creative side of it. I'm not in it for the glamour.*
>
> Sophie (talking about her job
> as fashion assistant)

Characteristic

Challenging Millennials involves continually exposing them to new learning.

Opportunity

Long-term financial benefits may not motivate them, but immediate and ongoing access to on-the-job learning will.

Threat

They may take that learning and use it elsewhere. But they will leave anyway and you can always buy that learning back, enriched by the insights they've gained applying it elsewhere.

Response

Forget classroom learning or tuition by rote (see Table 7.2). This generation's recreation – video, Internet and mobile phone games – includes learning. It is interactive and responsive to individual needs. Line managers need to be good coaches and good mentors. Learning needs to be on the job. Constant reviews, teasing out what can be personally gained from every experience, should be a matter of course. Teaching by action learning, scenario speculation, role-play and game-play – anything that adds a bit of life and fun – will always go down well, provided it is not aggressively competitive (remember, this is not Generation X) or too political (see below). See also 'Brainstorming Cool'.

Table 7.2 Growing up interactive

Broadcast learning (old style)	Interactive learning (new style)
Linear, sequential/serial	Hypermedia
Instruction	Construction and discovery
Teacher-centred	Learner-centred
Absorbing materials	Learning how to learn
School years	Lifelong
One-size-fits-all	Customized
Teacher as transmitter	Teacher as facilitator

Source: Don Tapscott (1998) *Growing Up Digital*

Examples

Channel Four

Channel Four, the UK's arts and niche entertainment channel, uses sophisticated e-learning software to induct its new professional staff. Channel Four is unique in the UK in being the only public sector organization that has to generate its own income and also unusual in that it does not produce any films or programmes itself.

The role of the managers who commission the programmes from independent production companies is therefore of critical importance. This not only covers interpreting the corporation's broadcasting strategy and policy but also determining fees and intellectual property rights as well as checking that the contracts meet the legal requirements of current government legislation.

This summary of the corporation's functions provides the focus for a new interactive intranet site launched in 1999, designed to familiarize new staff, who may have not experienced anything like this before, to the commissioning department. Sheila Robertson, then head of the channel's organizational development team, brought in e-learning software consultancy IQdos to design the training modules. On its recommendation she commissioned KMA Interactive Media to set up the intranet.

Robertson told KMA she wanted a product that would 'turn heads' in terms of improving skills and communication. This, the company responded, would necessitate a wide-ranging hardware upgrade, so the channel started installing new systems. A new post was created in organizational development so that one person could dedicate all their time to e-learning and the intranet.

The result has not only catapulted the HR department from the fringes of the organization to the centre but it has also broken new ground in creating self-paced intranet exercises that are fun as well as informative. Most popular of all has been a snakes and ladders game dreamt up by the business affairs department as a way of helping new recruits in the commissioning department to understand what it does.

A typical question in the game is:

> *You are commissioning editor for Channel Four television. A product company asks you whether it can set up a website to accompany the programme you are buying from it. Do you: (a) say that it's fine; (b) pass the query on to your business executive; or (c) email Channel Four's interactive department, saying that the production company has the online rights for the series?*
>
> *Move forward three paces if you chose (b). Move back two paces if you didn't.*

Jenny Tucker, assistant business affairs executive, was the contact point between the department and IQdos. The exercise is not, she argues, merely a cosmetic ice-breaker. The process of negotiating intellectual property rights is becoming more complicated and mistakes in the commissioning process can mean that the corporation lose the rights to the programmes it wants to make.

She also stresses the real importance of email tutors who know what they are doing and have been trained specifically for the task.[3] Julie Linn, e-learning manager for Britain's Training Foundation and a highly experienced trainer of e-tutors, concurs: 'A good e-tutor will fix problems before they arise and be at least one step ahead. They need to have the intuition to read between the lines – literally – in order to assess the student's progress at a distance without any of the tacit language available to the face-to-face trainer. Things can go pear-shaped very quickly – one minute everything is fine, the next a student can be ranting and raving.'[4]

St Barnado's

The head teacher of a local community primary school found that young single teachers working for the school were unable to mentally 'switch off' from their work at the end of the day because they felt unable to share issues and problems in the classrooms with their colleagues or senior teachers. Part of the problem was that there was little opportunity for the workforce as a whole to engage in joint social or development activity.

Accordingly one of the school's 'inset' (training) days was set aside for a team-building exercise. A training-needs analysis conducted by the work–life balance consultants organizing the event indicated that the majority of professional staff enjoyed out-of-hours socializing in pubs and bars. So the organizers hit on the idea of hiring a private room in a local bar and designing the team-building day around a series of traditional British pub games: darts, skittles, shove-halfpenny, quoits and table football.

Mixed groups of teachers and administrators were organized in teams and competed with each other in each of the games. During the activity, each team was asked to observe what role every member played. After the event, they were organized into syndicate groups to discuss the extent to which the roles adopted by each team member in the game (expert, supporter, coordinator etc.) corresponded to the role he or she played at work. In a final plenary session, the group examined how they could transfer the culture of support and encouragement they had demonstrated in the games to the workplace. 'This wasn't just good training. It was a great day out,' said one of the participants.[5]

TEAM BUILDING

> *Everybody's interests and obsessions seemed to cen-*
> *tre totally on a small circle of people at the office. Yet*
> *there was no loyalty between them at all.*
>> Owen (see 'The Provenance of Cool')

Characteristic

Millennials are loyal to their own and dislike disloyalty at work – intensely. Early contact with office politics, during school placements or college internships, is one of the most frequently-cited sources of disaffection with corporate employment.

Opportunity

If their loyalty to the task and the people can be won, their motivation will follow.

Threat

If their loyalty is taken for granted or undermined by power games, backstabbing or divide and rule tactics, you've lost them – mentally, physically or both.

Response

Establishing and maintaining team loyalty, always important, is paramount with Millennials. Project leaders or team managers need well-honed interpersonal and communication skills as well as integrity and an ability to influence others and productivity in the team. A participative management style is essential.

Example

Chris Byron was the manager chosen by British Airways to lead the team constructing their new Waterside headquarters. His ability to interpret the brief sensitively enough to meet the people needs of the building – so that the workspace design genuinely encouraged serendipity and cross-functional working – was largely due to his choice of team members and his collective approach to decision making.

Byron's choice of team members was an eclectic mix. He did not opt for the most obvious high-flyers but rather people whose enthusiasm for the project was based on intellectual engagement rather than corporate ladder climbing. Consequently, there was little homogeneity in their working style.

His leadership style needed to reflect this. It was on-site – as soon as progress permitted, the team worked from portakabins adjacent to the building – and very inclusive. Every member of the team was given the opportunity and, equally importantly, the time to make their contribution to the debate. Byron explains:

> We did not work to a rigid timescale. I did not try to drive things through like a professional chairman because railroading of this kind leaves a lack of real consensus that has a habit of jumping back at you further down the line. There were too many people with too many strong views and vested interests. Consequently, I adopted a more facilitating style, giving everyone a nominal time of five minutes to stress what issues they felt were at stake.
>
> Of course everyone took more time – up to fifteen minutes in many cases – but I was prepared to let the discussion go on if it contributed to our collective perspective.

> *Obviously I had to pull things together and ultimately make a decision but taking the time and patience to listen to the issues, sometimes for longer than I really wanted to, helps to create a common language in a team made up from very disparate backgrounds and disciplines.*

Where disagreement between team members raised issues of long-term significance, Byron would organize an 'away day' at a local hotel or business centre to thrash it out. This emphasis on consensus paid off. All the members of the former team are united in stressing that Byron's leadership style was critical in not only getting the project completed and on-budget but also in tapping the creative potential of the group.

'Over a period of time I became best buddies with people with whom I was as different as chalk and cheese,' says Alison Hartigan, one of the team. 'The respect for each other's knowledge – largely because Chris gave us the space and time we needed to acquire it – resulted in meetings in which collective insights were thrown up that seemed to come from nowhere. When there were disputes, Chris was incredibly good at problem solving. You were given the confidence to throw anything into the ring. You never had to preface your remark by asking whether it was a dumb remark.'[6]

VIRTUAL TEAMWORKING

Technology can be both an aid and a barrier to communication.

Andy Smith, Roffey Park Institute

Characteristic

Millennials are more comfortable than their peers in initiating, as well as sustaining, close personal and professional relationships at a 'physical' distance. They are likely to be attracted by flexible working arrangements that give them more freedom over where and when they undertake their work.

Opportunity

They make excellent virtual team members.

Threat

Keeping them motivated and coordinating their work is likely to be harder. Misunderstandings will sometimes occur because the nuances of facial and body language, which enhance face-to-face interactions, are not wholly replicable by current technology. This will be particularly true in the case of teams made up from mixed generations, where some members are less comfortable bonding at a distance than others.

Response

Line managers need to recruit team members on the basis of their self-starting skills and set objectives based on output and the ability to meet agreed objectives rather than 'clock-on, clock-off' time-worked performance. They need to encourage team members to be mutually supportive, but constantly check whether understandings of what has been agreed, said or assumed at a distance is the same between all parties.

Example

Save the Children used email to support quick and creative decision making during the humanitarian crisis caused by the recent war between Ethiopia and Eritrea.

The environment in which non-government organizations (NGOs) such as Save the Children operate is rarely static. It shifts with every change in local government policy, every new offensive by rebel or government forces, every crackdown on dissidents, every failed harvest or every move by a peripatetic, displaced population.

As a consequence, local officers in the field are the organization, in terms of creative decision making. Their insights and perspectives are the ones that count, particularly during periods of crisis, because they are the only people close enough to the situation to keep track of events that may change day by day or even hour by hour.

Email has revolutionized the way creative decisions are made. One Save the Children manager operating from the organization's headquarters in London described how, as recently as ten years ago, a little old lady with a tea trolley used to do the rounds of the offices twice a day handing out telex messages.

Now recommendations by local officers in the field can be acted on in minutes and strategies shaped and refined in a rapid and 'real time' interchange of messages – a critical factor when circumstances change, literally, minute by minute.

This was certainly the case in the emergency feeding programme put together by Save the Children in Eritrea during the war in May and June 2000, which won plaudits from both UNICEF and the Eritrean Ministry of Health.

Save the Children (SC) were able to move fast in setting up new feeding stations and in tracing tens of thousands of people displaced by the fighting because their 'man on the spot', programme officer Bruce MacInnes, acted on instinct in setting up an immediate appeal to SC's donors, without waiting for confirmation that the existing camps where the charity operated had been overrun by the Ethiopian army, and focused his attention on acquiring a new fleet of Land Rovers that would enable the charity to set up and continually resource the new camps.

From day one of the crisis, a continuous stream of emails criss-crossed the computer lines between MacInnes's office in Asmara, Save the Children's regional headquarters in Nairobi and the central headquarters in London.

Within two days of the crisis erupting, an initial appeal had been sent to the organization's donors. Within ten days chartered flights with the essential supplies and Land Rovers had touched down at Asmara airport. Six weeks after the Ethiopian invasion, ten feeding stations were operational, with three more due to open, serving a total of 25,000 hot, enriched meals a week to 3000 children and vulnerable women.

Monitoring the email traffic over this period enabled the authors to gauge first-hand the new dynamics email creates in shaping and sustaining ideas. A number of insights emerged, including the following.

A passway to inner thoughts
Bruce MacInnes is one of these managers that use email uninhibitedly. As his regional director Peter Hawkins observes: 'When Bruce thinks 'f**k', he writes 'f**k!' With few people to confide in and operating largely on his own after his local nutrition officer was repatriated, he used email as a medium to articulate his concerns and worries. His emails record his 'heart on sleeve' thoughts and contrast

with the clipped businesslike responses from managers in London and Nairobi, far away from the immediate sights and sounds of the crisis.

His reports to London were almost journalistic in their creative expression. At the end of the first full day of the crisis, he emailed his counterpart in London, Rachel Lambert: 'The one thing we know for sure is that the situation is fluid. It could change dramatically without warning, and accurate information is hard to come by. The atmosphere in town is tense. Much of the bombast [among the Eritreans about their military prospects] is gone as people settle down to the grim reality of this war.'

A few days later, thinking about what would happen when the fighting stopped, he added: 'The countryside will have bombed villages, razed homes, fields with land mines and unexploded ordnance and traumatized families coping with the loss of loved ones. Schools and health centres will be abandoned or piles of rubble.'

A conduit for support and advice

Just as MacInnes was able to articulate his needs, requirements and concerns in a manner that never would have been possible using old-fashioned technology, so managers in London and Nairobi were able to respond to these needs, both practically and emotionally, in a more immediate way using the same medium.

MacInnes exchanged emails with his counterpart in London, the emergency programme officer for East and Central Africa, Rachel Lambert, up to four to five times a day and sometimes almost continually. Together, they were able to put together a four-page security update for SC's donors within 24 hours of the crisis breaking. Over the next few days, a stream of traffic between London, Asmara and Nairobi allowed the strategy proposed by MacInnes to be shaped 'real time' by a stream of nutritional and health-care experts.

This enabled MacInnes's practical needs to be met. The emotional support was provided by Sarah Uppard, who at the time of the Eritrean crisis was the London-based emergency adviser for separated children. MacInnes and Uppard had worked closely together earlier in their careers. She was able to provide a constant stream of informal encouragement, once again using the medium of email as a conduit for uninhibited and spontaneous thoughts and humour in a way that would not have been possible on telex.

The email traffic between London and Asmara during the darkest days of the crisis, when MacInnes's creativity was being undermined by stress and overwork, was peppered with little messages from Uppard, such as 'I see you are faced with another emergency! Poor you – hope it goes OK,' when it became clear that several hundred children were separated from their parents in the camps or 'Gosh, you are on the ball … If only I had a little cloning factory turning out people like you!' when he had pulled off funding for another expat.

MILLENNIALS AS MANAGERS

A professional and assertive posture will help you fake a boss's mien until you actually develop one.
Meredith Keisner, executive director of FIRST
(Philadelphia, non-profit) at 25

Characteristics

Millennials bring to their role as managers a 'freshness' and 'realness' (see 'Cool Beginnings') that gives them an out-of-the-box perspective of what is and is not possible.

Opportunities

They are often excellent at creative ideas shaping and strategy development that helps build brand equity (see 'Cool Leadership'). They are usually more in touch with the trends, language and 'goz' that help shape consumer tastes and work-based attitudes.

Threats

They have no knowledge or experience of the ups and downs of long-term market conditions and often lack the skills needed to see work units or businesses as a whole through hard times. They often find it hard to establish their authority or identify with the needs of teams or work units comprising people of different ages and personal circum-stances (see 'Crux').

Response

Ensure that Millennials in management positions are prop-erly supported and advised by older mentors and senior executives that can temper their impulses and sustain their commitment as well as help establish their authority. Train Millennials to operate from a sophisticated management style, as follows:

- Monitor and alter supervisory styles based on the indi-vidual employee.
- Create a contextual leadership style where some deci-sions are made by the manager (with input) and others are consensus-driven.

- Create a place where power based on status or position is less important than personally earned influence and respect.
- Know how and when to make exceptions to the rule.
- Be thoughtful when forming teams and giving individuals assignments.
- Balance concern for tasks with concern for people.
- Create elements of trust, and work for it in your environment.[7]

Example

Susan Shin managed a staff of 90 'direct-reports' at Disney World's Epcot Centre in her early 20s. She won over veteran sceptics by selling them on the idea that if they were good to her, she'd make sure her bosses were good to them. Their success was tied to their ability to rise above the annoyance that they felt with Shin's lack of experience – and also their ability to recognize that she was the work unit's most effective 'resource gatherer', able by her authority and energy to negotiate back-up that they lacked access to. 'Good leaders are judged by the way they react,' she concludes.

Donning the leadership mantle at an early age also nearly always involves run-ins with former peers. Peter Beinhart says he suddenly had to maintain a formal and reserved distance from his long-time friends when he became their editor at the US political journal *The New Republic* in 2000, aged 28. Before his promotion he was just another senior editor who occasionally filled in as boss. But now he had power over them. 'Since you're privy to sensitive information about other people, shooting your mouth off will make people nervous in a way it wouldn't before,' he says.

In fact, he knows more than he wants to know. One time he knew that a friend and co-worker would have a hard time breaking personal obligations if Beinhart assigned him a late-breaking story. But the journalist was essential so Beinhart 'the boss' supplanted Beinhart 'the friend'. The friend did the job and cancelled his personal plans.[8]

Beinhart's instinct – to take a step back from the collegial group of peers – was the right one, according to Bruce Tulgan, author of *Managing Generation Y*.[9] A new Millennial-age manager should err on the side of formality. Be nice and charming, he says, but always remember that pushing people to get things done is your job.

BRAINSTORMING COOL

8

Grammar is disappearing – this is the first generation which is creating its own language with icons and mobile phones.

Martin Lindstrom, author, *Brandchild*

Creative exchanges are often formalized into 'brainstorms'. Groups engage in an uninhibited flow of thoughts and ideas. The key rules (see guidelines below) are that it is the volume of ideas that counts, not their perceived quality, that participants build on each other's ideas, rather than claiming them as their 'own' and that everybody suspends judgement: there is no 'wrong' idea.

Millennials are great at this. They have grown up taking part in electronic chatlines, mobile phone text exchanges and interactive video games that reproduce exactly this dynamic. Where there is unwelcome constraint, it usually comes from the organization, not the individual.

What's involved?

LANGUAGE

Characteristic

Millennials play around with language. They introduce phrases or words from the latest films or music ('smoking', 'shagtastic', 'dissing') and enliven them by juxtaposition or prefixing ('cheese-eating surrender monkeys', 'ground-his-bones-into-dust-kinda-dead'). They have also played around with interactive fantasy, engaging in 'what if' scenarios and 'let's see what happens' exercises on video and mobile phone games.

Opportunity

Experienced brainstormers use words and phrases to open up new trains of thought, allowing team members to see the problem from a different perspective. Playing around with reality is part and parcel of the process.

Threat

Just as no single idea is good or bad, no 'what if' scenario is stupid or implausible. Any discussion needs to avoid value judgements.

Examples

Exercises that are likely to appeal to Millennial thinking include 'ideal if', which raises the sights of the group by asking, in their particular situation, what would constitute an ideal solution and then explore means of achieving it. Or 'metaphor', which asks the group to express what the issue they are discussing is 'like'. An old-fashioned example would be 'the lack of accurate marketing data means the company is like a bird of prey with a squint'. A Millennial-generation example would be that the lack of accurate marketing data means the company was 'a fiscal flatliner, operating on antique circuits' (actual description of a magazine out of touch with its readers in *New Yorker*, 9 March 1992).

HUMOUR

Characteristic

Millennials use humour to break down online barriers. It says something important about an individual on the other end of the terminal when there's no facial expressions or body language to go on. Live comedy is as popular as live music.

Opportunity

Experienced brainstormers use humour to break down barriers between group members and to help people start freewheeling. Wild ideas are also encouraged, off-the-wall or, as a Millennial might put it 'definitely not white-bread'.

It's worth stressing here that, as we discussed in 'The Provenance of Cool', the ability to understand and produce humour requires the complex interplay of several thought processes: working memory (holding a piece of information in mind while you manipulate it); cognitive shifting (looking at a situation in different ways or from different perspectives) and abstract thinking.

Research at the University of Toronto links the ability to laugh at the complex analogies and ironies of an Eddie Izzard monologue or a comic exchange in *Friends* with the frontal lobe of the brain. 'The frontal lobe is important because it is the part of the brain that gets the most information from the rest of the brain,' explains Toronto's Professor Prathiba Shammi. 'It brings together information from the thinking part of the brain with the emotional part of the brain.'

Threat

Humour can sometimes offend. Some level of team affinity (see 'Managing Millennials') will help to anticipate the cultural hot points.

Example

An old-style warm-up exercise would be 'How many uses are there for a paperclip?' One Millennial-style response would be 'So that you can accidentally staple your tongue to the wall' ('It hurt the way your tongue hurts after you accidentally staple it to the wall' was a description in a recent GSCE exam essay – see p. 42).

REMOTE BRAINSTORMING

Characteristic

Millennials are used to being uninhibited at a distance. They can establish electronically excellent one-to-one and group rapport that their parents or elder siblings might find hard to achieve.

Opportunity

Researchers at the Massachusetts Institute of Technology (MIT) recently tested new software designed to support electronic brainstorming. The tests, involving 800 people, found that the creative output from electronic brainstorming sessions was greater than those conducted face to face – and that, furthermore, these productivity gains increased along with the size of group.[1] This was because in face-to-face sessions, the most assertive and outgoing members of the group dominated the exchange, with quieter but equally insightful individuals keeping their thoughts to themselves.

Threat

In practice, however, the capacity of email to free up thought in the organization depends on two interrelated factors: the extent to which individuals feel comfortable with email and the Internet as a creative medium and the way exchanges are monitored or regulated by the organization. The level of software policing currently undertaken by many organizations is wholly antipathetic to the process of uninhibited 'freewheeling' that brainstorming entails – and that Millennials are used to in personal exchanges at home.

Examples

The phrase 'sexing up' – to describe political spin-doctoring of documents – was recently 'rejected' in an article submitted by a freelance journalist to a top business journal because the word 'sex' was not 'allowed' by the software. So was a reference to the top TV series *Sex in the City*. A respected academic researcher conducting a survey into recruitment screening could not file his work under the term 'AIDS' because the words 'AIDS' and 'HIV positive' were 'prohibited'. What kind of Orwellian planet do these digital security experts live on?

BRAINSTORMING IN PRACTICE: EXAMPLE

In 'Inside Cool', a brief reference was made to the creative exchanges that take place at the Californian design company IDEO.

Few companies, for example, practice brainstorming with the frequency, intensity or sincerity as IDEO, one of the world's leading industrial design firms. The Palo Alto-based company, founded by David Kelley in 1978, has launched a stunningly diverse range of products, ranging from the Polaroid I-Zone Camera to Crest Toothpaste's Neat Squeeze tube.

The firm's designers and engineers – drawn largely from Stanford University – use brainstorming as their principal means of tapping collective thought. 'Brainstorming is practically a religion at IDEO, one we practice every day,' says Tom Kelley, David's brother and the firm's general manager. 'Brainstorming is the idea engine of our culture.'

Yet Kelley stresses that most organizations that try to emulate what IDEO does are merely going through the motions. 'The problem with brainstorming is that everybody thinks they already do it. When I raise the topic at presentations and in conversations with business executives, I see some eyes start to glaze over with the smug "been there, done that" look.'

Among the more important principles underlying IDEO's approach to brainstorming are:

- A questioning attitude. Design teams are expected to make mistakes early and often. Coming to the 'right' solution too quickly is discouraged. People are encouraged to question any and all assumptions about what innovation means. In IDEO's culture you aren't innovative unless you are challenging the client's, the team's and your own pre-existing notions. Paradoxically this means that, during brainstorms, any notions other than standard company or industry orthodoxies are given an open hearing.

- Intellectual diversity. Every design has trade-offs and the firm understands that truly diverse teams will question which ones make the most sense. Diversity in brainstorming is encouraged so teams will make the right kind of arguments about the right kind of trade-offs. 'Without the rigours of competing passions, fully expressed, the end result is likely to feel arbitrary and political, not at all like the inspiring inevitability of effective surprise, and probably not very cost-effective either,' says Kelley.

Kelley argues that innovation is not just about surprising ideas. It is about surprising people – and that fostering innovation is mainly about encouraging people to relate to each other in creative ways. However creative an individual is, his or her contribution is useless unless the team can work with it. 'Being a design genius is great,' he concludes, 'but being a design genius at the expense of the team is not.'[2]

THE FIVE-STEP WAY TO BRAINSTORMING

The purpose of this exercise is to place a creative group in discussion in an environment where a free flow of ideas is not interrupted by censorious or judgemental comments from any member.

The two most important principles of brainstorming are the focus on the volume of ideas rather than their coherence – because even if an idea is wild and impractical it may act as a bridge to one that is original but workable – and that nothing should be said or implied that cuts off the inspirational source of this flow.

Thus the five guidelines that should govern any brainstorm are:

- Everyone should suspend judgment. Anything goes – there is no wrong idea.
- Participants should 'freewheel'. They should 'drift and dream' their way around the problem rather than analysing every thought.
- The volume of ideas is what counts. One thought acts as a stimulus to another and any attempt to order or rationalize them on the basis of their relevance or appropriateness will cut off the creative flow.
- 'Hitch-hiking' should be encouraged. Participants should build on each other's ideas, abandoning any attempt to 'own' or protect any idea that emerges from the discussion.
- Wild ideas are welcome. These are the ones that are most likely to break the mould, however unworkable or ridiculous they may seem.

A suggested approach

- State the problem the group will consider and engage in preliminary discussion to find out whether some members of the group see it differently. Out of this discussion, two or three 'statements' or definitions may emerge. Note these on the flipchart.
- Select one of these 'statements' as the focus for the brainstorm. It is important that this is done with the consensus of the whole team.
- Warm up the team by trying out their brainstorming skills on a light-hearted subject, to encourage laughter and help people start 'freewheeling'. A common exercise used by creative teams is 'How many uses are there for a paperclip (or a brick)?'

- The main brainstorm then begins. During the exercise, the team can opt to use a variety of techniques to open up new trains of thought or allow team members to see the problem from a different perspective. These include reverse brainstorming, 'ideal if', metaphor, structured daydreaming and wildest ideas. Details of all of these are set out below. Remember also to follow the dos and don'ts, also set out below. It is common for brainstorms to end with a 'wildest idea' session and this is recommended.
- In a final session, summarize the ideas generated that the team wish to pursue or use. Again, it is important that all team members agree on these.

Dos and don'ts of brainstorming

Do:

- encourage noise;
- encourage laughter;
- allow silly ideas;
- conduct the brainstorm in the spirit of the five guidelines set out above;
- enforce, in particular, the requirement that all participants suspend judgment on any idea generated, however wild and seemingly impractical;
- have a warm-up session to encourage laughter and help everyone to start freewheeling;
- number all ideas serially;
- end up on the wildest idea.

Don't:

- tape-record – it makes everyone self-conscious and inhibits a free flow of thought;
- use blackboards or transparencies – for similar reasons;
- allow observers;
- accept interruptions;
- flip over completed flipchart sheets – tear off the sheets and stick them to the wall using blue-tack so they remain visible and fresh in everyone's mind;
- spend too long on initial discussion or allow too much detail;
- prolong a session beyond its useful life.

BRAINSTORMING TECHNIQUES

Reverse brainstorming

This is used to test the robustness of any solution arrived at through an exchange of wild ideas, particularly if it is to be implemented by other departments or senior management. The question to be asked and discussed is: In what ways can this idea fail? This will help the group's members prepare answers to difficult questions and deal with potential problems before the event.

Ideal if

This technique is most useful when group members are just starting to address the issues. Before participants get locked too tightly into their current way of thinking, the question is put: With this problem and its solution, what would be the most ideal outcome? This lifts the discussion beyond a constrained and often negative perspective to a more positive sense of what is possible. Everyone is, so to speak, lifted by a couple of notches – and while we are on the subject of analogy ...

Metaphor

This technique has many forms, but one of the most useful is that a member of the group with an issue to raise outlines the essential problem and then asks the group to suggest a metaphor that most resembles it. In a recent discussion about ways in which non-executive directors could be used more effectively, for example, a director on the board of a UK lottery company described the need for better induction by saying that he felt his role was like that of a bidet: nobody knows what it is for but it adds a touch of class to the bathroom!

A list of ten metaphors for each problem should be gathered and the group then focuses down to two or three that it would like to work with and uses these as a starting point to help them get deeper into the problem – for example, the 'bidet' analogy forced the group to look more closely at the extent to which NEDs are used by cynical CEOs as window dressing for the company's investors.

If the group is having difficulty getting started, two supplementary questions can be used to break the ice: What aspect of nature does the problem most resemble? (e.g. a company with too much bureaucracy is like a river clogged with bindweed); or, if we were the problem, how would the world look to us? (e.g. a bank that fails to finance our project is merely protecting the money of its existing clients).

Reversal

This technique is useful if a group member is, or group members are, stuck in the problem being dealt with. It asks: What if we opted for the opposite course? For example, 'What if we kept the old, less expensive but more inefficient supplier rather than the new one proposed? Would we be able to use the money we save to build internal safeguards to make up for the deficiency?'

These apparently simple questions can often trigger new ways of looking at the problem.

Structured daydreaming

This technique is another method for generating energy and novel solutions. It has to be led either by the group leader or by one of the group taking on the role of discussion leader.

The particular question or problem is written up on the flipchart for all to see. The leader then tells the group to shut their ideas and leads them by gentle questioning to construct images of where they find themselves in their mind's eye.

Several changes of scene are gone through. After members of the group have opened their eyes, the central images are written or drawn up and are used as a starting point for discussion.

This is another technique for tapping deep into the imagination but it needs familiarity to run successfully. It is best attempted with a group that has brainstormed successfully together on a number of occasions.

Wildest ideas

We tend always to tread cautiously, either consciously or unconsciously, in putting forward new ideas that may seem impractical. This technique gives members of the group un-limited licence to come up with totally unworkable ideas.

In this session, no 'workable' ideas can be proposed. The effect is to help members of the group to suspend judgement on the ideas of others (which, as we have seen, is vital in effective brainstorming). It also gives everyone direct access to the deepest recesses of their imagination in a way no other technique achieves.

BRANDING COOL

9

Despite the fact that *Marketing Week*, quite rightly, points out the contradictions of a branding strategy based on a youth counterculture that loathes consumerism and all it stands for (see 'Outside Cool'), 'cool' image building has worked for a number of companies that have been careful to avoid the traps. Eternally 'cool' brands such as Jack Daniels, Adidas and Volkswagen show what is possible – but the process is continuous and unforgiving. If you are trading on street credibility, you cannot sit on your laurels.

Companies as varied as Puma, Vespa and Burberry boosted their sales in the 1990s through slick advertising and close association with models and celebrities who cut ice with affluent Generation X professionals – only to find they lacked the staying power to re-position the brand to a breed of Generation Y youngsters with very different values. The challenge of inter-generational re-branding nearly ruined Levi's and is currently testing Coca-Cola to the limit. And Hilfiger, the company that took Levi's to the cleaners in the late 1990s (see 'Outside Cool'), is now facing problems of its own as the next generation of consumers move away from department stores – where Hilfiger has a collarhold – back to boutiques.

In 'The Provenance of Cool' and 'Outside Cool', we cited a number of characteristics of Millennials that distinguished them from their Generation X predecessors. Let's summarize what impact some of these characteristics may have in brand equity terms.

INTERACTIVE WORLDS

Characteristic

Fantasy is now interactive. Previously static, hand-me-down alternative worlds such as Middle Earth (in *Lord of the Rings*), *Dune* and *Alien* are being revitalized. Newly created ones such as *Lara the Tomb Raider* are interactive from the start.

Opportunity

Internet, video and mobile phone games open up a whole new medium for advertising and brand building. People tend to play games for long periods. Many games are initially released in 'demo' form, a limited version of the game that is given away as a teaser to encourage users to buy a full version when it appears. Ads placed in demos could count the days until the game's release, provide a link to an online store for advance orders and switch to promoting other games from the same vendor once the game comes out.

Threat

Many games makers are reluctant to dilute their brands with other firms' ads. It has not proved popular with users who see their interactive worlds contaminated with commercial intrusions.

Response

Traditional advertising based on the characters from video games has proved successful. The Lucozade campaign in the late 1990s was a template. Lara Croft from the *Tomb*

Raider games flees through an underground cavern from a pack of pursuing dogs, only to find her way blocked by a chasm. Cornered, she reaches over her shoulder into her backpack, retrives a bottle of Lucozade and drinks its contents. Revitalized, she gives the dogs the slip and sprints to safety.

Conducent, a company based in Harrisburg, Pennsylvania, took things a stage further in the early 2000s. It pioneered selling screen space on Internet games to such advertisers as Amazon, Lycos and Egghead. Ads can appear before or after a game, or between episodes of gameplay (such as after losing a life). Crucially, they can be configured so that clicking on an ad calls up the advertiser's website. Details of the number of times an advert is placed, and whether or not it was clicked on, are also recorded and passed back to Conducent.

Conducent foresees a future where games and other software are supported by advertising, sponsorship or even product placement (see the example of NeoPets in 'The Provenance of Cool'). Since this would make software cheaper, or even free, consumers might live with this, according to Forrester Research, a top US market research agency. But the word to stress here is 'live with'. Whether cross-selling or sponsorship of this kind proves a viable source of long-term brand equity is still an 'out of court' issue.

HUMOUR AND LANGUAGE

Characteristic

Humour has been a cornerstone of teenage culture, boosted by a revolution in the way language is used, orally and verbally.

Opportunity

Irony, self-deprecation and plain speaking have replaced old-style image building.

Threat

The language you think may be their language may not be.

Response

Straight talking works wonders. Sprite has scored with ads that parody celebrity endorsers and carry the tagline 'Image is nothing. Obey your thirst'. J.C. Penney & Co.'s hugely successful Arizona Jeans brand has a new campaign showing teens mocking ads that attempt to speak their language. The tagline? 'Just show me the jeans.'

However, learn also from BP's attempt at irony. Following its acquisition of US competitors Amoco and Arco, it decided that the 'British' in its name was a burdensome legacy from an imperial past. However, a brief flirtation with ads announcing 'Beyond Petroleum' was abandoned abruptly; some folk apparently thought this was the company's official name.

IKEA, the Swedish furniture manufacturer, got the balance of targeted humour and language smack on the nose when it developed a brochure for cheap and cheerful chairs and sofas aimed at young buyers setting up home or in college digs for the first time. The circular, printed in bright primary colours, adopted the editorial style of teenage fanzines and focussed on the teen phrase 'schlomping', describing the laid back way in which Millennials sprawl all over their parents' furniture while watching television or listening to CDs.

The front-page title 'Schlomping: The Live UnLtd trend that gives formal sitting the heave-ho' sets the scene for the rest of the brochure. It offered footstools for 'feet-up schlomping', moulded plastic garden bucket chairs for 'alfresco schlomping', wicker recliners for 'laid-back conservatory schlomping' and a stuffed rocker for 'junior schlomping'.

A screaming headline announcing that 'Career girls schlomp too!' is the backdrop for 'Marilyn', sitting with laptop in hand and announcing 'After a hard day climbing the corporate ladder, I like nothing more than to surf for shoes on my POANG armchair'. Meanwhile, her generously proportioned auntie is sitting on a KLACKBO easy chair under the announcement 'Big-booty schlomping: schlomping furniture for all kinds of behinds'. Finally, a tangle of legs and arms emerging from a yellow, red and pink stripy duvet forms the backdrop for the announcement 'Push two KLIPPAN sofas together for some seriously silly late-night schlomping.'

The use of 'references' is particularly clever. Phrases such as 'After a hard day climbing the corporate ladder, I like nothing more than' and, later in the brochure, 'Fact: schlomping allows more blood flow to the brain, making you up to 43% smarter – if you're sceptical, take these tests' are a piss-take of the adverts Millennials had to sit through in their parents' house while growing up. The entire strategy uses Millennial-age play on words to appeal to young adults who want furniture that suits their needs and not those of their parents at a time when they can give vent to them for the first time.

AWARENESS

Characteristic

Millennials are cause-driven, unlike their more detached Generation X predecessors.

Opportunity

The emerging fashionable doctrine of the decade is 'cause branding'. In the US, companies have put their names and resources to work supporting worthy causes deliberately to enhance their reputations, deepen employee loyalty, strengthen ties with business partners and even sell more products and services. According to a recent study on good corporate citizenship commissioned by Cone, a Boston-based consulting firm specializing in cause branding and marketing, 88 per cent of employees feel 'a strong sense of loyalty' to their employers. As many as 53 per cent of employees in the survey stated that they actually chose to work at the organizations partly because of their employers' expressed commitment to high-profile social issues. Consumers, according to the survey, increasingly shop with a cause in mind and consider a company's support of social causes when deciding which products to buy and recommend to others.

Threat

The cause has to reflect the values and culture of the company. Millennials' hypocrisy barometers are more finely tuned than those of their parents or elder siblings.

Response

ConAgra, the US food giant, is a good example of a company that got it right. The company has embraced the cause of
combating child hunger by underwriting 100 after-school
cafes now serving about one million hot meals each year.
The programme, called Feeding Children Better, also encourages employees to raise money and serve meals, donates products and food trucks across the United States,
and leads a national public-service advertising campaign
to raise public awareness of child hunger.

By contrast, Coca-Cola, in another example of the de-
fensive wrong-footed way it has tried to sustain its brand
image in recent years, got cause branding badly wrong. Its
recent attempts to ally itself with the US Institute of Paedi-
atric Dentistry raised howls of hyprocrisy from consumers
and workers alike (see 'Outside Cool').

24/7 LIVING

Characteristic

Millennials club. They have a hedonistic attitude to 24/7
living. Whether as students or single professionals, they
live late and play late.

Opportunity

Late-night living opens up the opportunity for new style
fashions and branding.

Threat

It's still a new frontier with trends and values that are still emerging. Decisions are still being made by instinct rather than on the basis of comprehensive market research.

Response

There are few better examples of cool hunting than the way in which the newly-merged Diageo company turned around the ailing market for spirits in the late 1990s by jumping on the clubbing bandwagon. Focusing its market research attentions on both the new bottle-swigging habits of beer drinkers and the (then) current craze for 'alcopops' (sweet fizzy drinks with a strong kick) it came up with a series of ready mixed cocktails based on its core spirits of vodka and whiskey.

The resulting re-branding of Smirnoff, based around two derivative bottled mixes – Smirnoff Ice (vodka and lemon) and Smirnoff Mule – was a huge success, with the company enhancing the brand through a series of sponsor-ships of concerts, festivals and club events. In London, the company also sponsors free travel on public transport on New Year's Eve, in the knowledge that the majority of night-time travellers are Millennial-age clubbers. In the wake of current plans by the Greater London Authority to extend West End tube and bus travel into the small hours every weekend (see 'Outside Cool'), Smirnoff is considering how they can build on the success of this campaign

Not all of these strategies work. A parallel campaign to re-brand Bells whisky proved a damp squib. The equiva-lent to Smirnoff Ice, a tinned mixture of Bells and Irn-Bru, a medicinal soft drink popular in Scotland, did not take. A supporting television advertisment campaign suggesting Bells was a sexy drink for young adults attracted flack from regulators.

The hit/miss nature of Diageo's spirits campaigns illustrates the dilemma of 'cool' branding. It's a trial and error
process with no guarantee of success. The recent successful Fanta drinks advertisement campaign scored big-time.
The backing track was taken up by underground DJs, the
ultimate street credibility. But the creative director of the
advertising agency that came up with the formula, Brian
Crouch, warns against trying 'to add cool to something that
doesn't want to accept it', particularly in the drinks sector.
There was no rigorous scientific formula behind the Fanta
campaign, he stresses. Its flavour and tone was one based
on instinct with no more justification to it other than 'we
felt it was right'.

SUMMARY

COOL BEGINNINGS

- Millennials – 18 to 25-year-olds born after 1980 who are now active workers and consumers – are the first generation that wholly lacks the psychological baggage of a post-World War II social contract based on a guaranteed job for life and pension.
- Growing up with a rattle in one hand and a computer mouse in the other has given Millennials not just a practical mastery that usually exceeds that of their parents or elder siblings but also a psychological affinity that will dramatically extend the boundaries of how Internet and third-generation mobile phone technology is used as a day-to-day business medium.
- But this isn't just about technological prowess. Inspired by hit television series such as *Friends* and *Buffy the Vampire Slayer*, Millennials stick together as a group far more than their Generation X predecessors, whose key characteristic was ironic detachment.
- This presents both employers and brand managers with a distinct challenge. The social networks built up by most Millennials by the time they are young adults owes far less to mainstream corporate culture than those of their parents or elder siblings at the same age. A far higher proportion of these networks is likely to be made up of peers who are home-based free agents, who regard old-fashioned brand image building with suspicion and

whose social (as well as professional) lives do not revolve around a constant, all-encompassing workplace.

THE PROVENANCE OF COOL

- Examining the formative influences they were most likely to have been exposed to, they are entering employment with the following cultural make-up:
  - a strong sense of corporate employment as being senseless, hypocritical and boring;
  - an iconography that stresses a feminine take on society, loyalty to your own self- made community and the ability to be freestanding and shape your own worlds;
  - a perspective on the world, shaped by increasingly cross-cultural influences, that is multi-ethnic and global;
  - a wholly iconoclastic and irreverent use of language, marked by humour and vivid imagery;
  - a set of expectations in which there are no longer any benefits in playing safe.
- It is not that the general sense of corporate employment being seen from a distance as boring, useless and divisive is any different from the picture we had as teenagers. It is that this impression has been reinforced, not dispelled, by negative depictions in the media over the 1990s (*The Office, Jerry Maguire, Wall Street*); and by first-hand feedback or second-hand impressions of their parents and elder siblings under stress, during a decade when the post-World War II social contract of a job for life and a safe pension was not just questioned but blown out of the water.

OUTSIDE COOL

Cool hunting is neither new nor universally applicable. It dates back to the first attempts to explain and target youth counterculture in the 1960s. Then, as now, it was consumer and advertising led. Terms like 'yuppie', 'wigger', 'metrosexual' and 'freeter' have influenced how social trends in the past four decades have been popularly seen and interpreted – but they focus primarily on how people behave as consumers. We have tried to intepret the broader attitudes and behaviours of Millenials through a number of key words:

- *Intimacy*: In contrast to the two previous generations, Millennials grew up with Internet and mobile phone technology as a primary means of communicating with their friends and peers. Again, in contrast to boomers and Generation X, they commonly use these technologies to initiate relationships as well as (as is more usually the case with older people) sustaining relationships that have already been forged face to face. This has the potential to transform the way in which work-based networks and customer relations are conducted in the future. Firms that are fully part of the 'new economy' will be distinguished by their ability to exploit this.
- *Loyalty*: Millennials' primary loyalty is to an immediate social circle that is entirely of their own creation and, far more than was the case in previous generations, owes little or nothing to mainstream corporate culture. This means that, both in terms of recruitment or retention and brand marketing or product development, corporations are working strictly from the outside and are heavily reliant on focus group feedback and attitude-based field

research to inform campaigns directly targeted at teen-agers and young adults.

- *Awareness*: Precisely because they have been on the re-ceiving end of up to 20,000 commercial messages a year, Millennials are far more aware of circumstances when they are being deliberately manipulated and have a far lower tolerance of cant and hypocrisy. Traditional brand awareness strategies simply do not work. Millennials are far more likely to respond to campaigns (recruit-ment or brand marketing) based on irony, humour and unvarnished truth rather than on sophisticated image building. The growing field of cause branding, where a company's image and staff relations are transformed by a focused support for needy social causes, will only work if there is a clear link between the firm's values and cul-ture and its professed social ideals.

- *Balance*: Millennials have been at the cutting edge of 24/7 living. Unlike previous generations, who have extended family and professional responsibilities into 'unsocial' hours reluctantly under time pressures, unattached young adults (fast-laners) have actively embraced the 24-hour culture. Their view is hedonistic and bound up with the immediate satisfaction of their wants. As a re-sult, they have fuelled the development of new evening and night-time economies, particularly in the UK, which over time will open up employment and commercial op-portunities to a broader cross-section of society.

- *Risk*: Perceptions of Millennials as baggage-less free agents have been subject to some change in recent years. This view was US-led and heavily influenced by the American-generated economic boom of the 1990s and the turn of the century dot.com bubble. When this bubble burst in 2001 and the economy plateaued, this heady optimism collapsed. Millennials are undoubtedly free of the cultural attachment boomers and Generation X had to the post-World War II promises of a job for life and pension-based security. But their aspirations and capabilities as entrepreneurial free thinkers are largely determined by local cultural influences, social circumstances and family mores.

INSIDE COOL

Reviewing how employers best respond to the challenge of attracting and keeping a new generation of independent baggage-free and unsettled workers, it becomes clear that many of the strategies consist of measures that they should be doing anyway – only better. They include:

- Introducing ideas-generation and team working methods that will mentally engage Millennials with bright ideas and keep them that way.
- Making spotting and championing good ideas among their staff an essential management role – one that is built into their job specification and that they are appraised by.
- Taking advantage of Millennials' comfort with Internet-based technology by introducing maximum flexibility in where work is undertaken – something that will also help them reconcile and integrate the work they undertake for the organization with their broader 24/7 lives.
- Ridding intranet and incoming Internet exchanges of the kind of policing that will undermine the very spontaneity and uninhibitedness that Millennials are best able to offer.
- Reviewing the way employee communications and strategy reporting is undertaken to ensure that it is up to date and reflects the reality on the ground.

- Helping individuals link work with the organization with other 'third place' activities that provide them with sources of self-fulfilment and self-expression – including supporting charitable causes on company time, offering imaginative patterns of work and offering the opportunity to help launch company-funded enterprise spin-offs.

CRUX

Many of the attitudes and characteristics of Millennials are likely to change over time. They may be deferring some of the baggage of adult life – marriage or committed co-habitation, parenthood, property ownership – later than their parents or elder siblings. But these aspirations are still there. They may have little or no faith in the traditional altars of social security – a lifetime job or a safe pension – but they will find some way of putting resources aside for their old age. But there are some beliefs and behaviours from their childhood that are not likely to change and which have disturbing implications for current business practice.

- Millennials have grown up more actively engaged in the shaping and execution of public policy than any previous generation. They are surprisingly well informed on some of the key issues facing business and society, including international corporate social policy, environmental resource management and political and business governance and leadership. Their attitudes towards the ethics and currently accepted boundaries governing the social role and responsibilities of businesses are likely to revolutionize issues as varied as the use of child labour, the responsibilities that accompany global investment and the interface between government and commerce.

- Internet and third-generation mobile phone technology is transforming the way ideas and their creative output are disseminated, on a scale that has not been seen since the invention of the printing press. Social and commercial innovation has profited from this but the measures currently in place to protect its long-term financial returns have been fatally undermined in the process. Millennials, and many of their parents, simply do not accept the current boundaries. The law governing patents, intellectual copyright and brand protection will need to be reviewed to reflect this.
- The great challenge over the next two decades will be to create management and employment practices that cross different generations. This might include learning about employees the way that companies currently learn about their customers, shaping the workplace around their needs, creating a variable leadership style where some decisions are made by the manager and others are consensus-driven and encouraging lateral career movement between different work units, work patterns and parts of the organization.

COOL LEADERSHIP

The dot.com crash of 2001 has taken some of the hype and gloss away from the image of the Millennial entrepreneur. Nevertheless, a number of more durable 'truths' remain:

- Successful entrepreneurs who start their businesses young are closer to the market and more capable of creating a brand with an identity that will appeal to the latest market. That is what they bring to the business. They are generally not natural born managers and usually sensible enough to recognize it.

- The determining factor is not the launch or the early start-up but the roll out. To succeed, the entrepreneur brings in an experienced professional to tackle the implications of the growth. But the roles are different and not to be confused. The role of the executive is to consolidate the business. The role of the entrepreneur is to keep looking for new markets and keep the brand fresh.
- Nonetheless, naivety is no bad thing in organizational terms if it uses simple 'why' questions to confront entrenched thinking and outdated practices.

REFERENCES

1 COOL BEGINNINGS

1 Simon Caulkin, 'A brand new kind of advert', *The Observer*, 6 April 2003.
2 Jean Lammiman and Michel Syrett (2000) *Entering Tiger Country: How Ideas are Shaped in Organisations,* Roffey Park Institute.
3 Charlene Marmer Solomon (2000) 'Ready or not, here come the net kids', *Workforce*, February.
4 Karen Vella-Zarb (2000) 'Meet the future: it's your kids', *Fortune*, 24 July.
5 Don Tapscott and Nicholas Brealey (1998) *Growing Up Digital: The Rise of the Net Generation*, McGraw-Hill.
6 Chris Anderson (2000) 'Know Future', from 'Bright Young Things: A Survey of the Young', *The Economist*, 23 December.
7 Opinion Research Council Survey, 2000.
8 Chris Anderson (2000) 'Bright Young Things: A Survey of the Young', *The Economist*, 23 December.
9 Ibid, p. 8.
10 Bruce Tulgan (2001) *Managing Generation Y*, HRD Press.
11 Janet Wiscombe (2002) 'Layoffs hit younger workers', *Workforce*, March.
12 Karen Vella-Zarb (2000) 'Meet the future: it's your kids', *Fortune*, 24 July.
13 Andy Smith and Annette Sinclair (2003) *What Makes an Excellent Virtual Manager?* Roffey Park Institute.
14 'Creative licence', *People Management*, 20 March 2003, pp. 30–33.
15 *People Management*, 6 February 2002, p. 15.
16 'Generation Y: the graduates who dare ask for more', *The Times*, 17 April 2003.
17 Chris Anderson (2000) 'Bright Young Things: A Survey of the Young', *The Economist*, 23 December.
18 Jonas Ridderstråle and Kjell Nortdström (2000) *Funky Business*, Financial Times/Prentice Hall.

2   THE PROVENANCE OF COOL

1   Irvine Welsh (1996) *Trainspotting*, Minerva.
2   Michel Syrett and Jean Lammiman (2002) *Successful Innovation: How to Encourage and Shape Profitable Ideas*, Economist Books.
3   Carol Kennedy (2001) *The Next Big Idea: Managing in the Digital Age*, Random House, p. 129.
4   'Making companies efficient: the year downsizing grew up,' *The Economist*, 21 December 1996, pp. 115–17.
5   Michel Syrett (1997) 'Goodbye to macho management', *Director*, March, p. 49.
6   Douglas Coupland (1991) *Generation X: Tales for an Accelerated Culture*, Minerva.
7   Tom Wolfe (1998) *Bonfire of the Vanities*, Cape.
8   Martin Lindstrom (2003) *Brandchild,* Kogan Page.
9   'Advertisers reach Generation Y through NeoPets web community', *Direct Marketing*, March 2001.
10 Karen Vella-Zarb (2000) 'Meet the future: it's your kids', *Fortune*, 24 July.
11 Ibid.
12 Elizabeth Knowles with Juliet Elliott (eds) (1997) *The Oxford Dictionary of New Words*, Oxford University Press.
13 *The Face*, September 1993, p. 152.
14 *New Yorker*, 9 March 1992, p. 30.
15 *Spy*, May 1992, p. 60.

3   OUTSIDE COOL

1   Thomas Frank (1997) *The Conquest of Cool: Business Culture, Counterculture and the Rise of Hip Consumerism*, University of Chicago Press.
2   Malcolm Gladwell (2003) *The Tipping Point: How Little Things Can Make a Big Difference*, Little Brown.
3   'Cool for Cash', *Marketing Week*, 15 August 2002, pp. 24–7.
4   London Business School (2002) *Business Review*, Autumn.
5   Michel Syrett and Jean Lammiman (2002) *Creativity*, Capstone Publishing, ExpressExec series, p. 27.
6   'Strong players', *The Economist*, 14 December 2002, p. 72.
7   Michel Syrett and Jean Lammiman (2002) *Creativity*, Capstone Publishing, ExpressExec series, pp. 27–30.
8   Sanders & Sydney (2000) *Friendship Works*, Sanders & Sydney.
9   Martin Lindstrom (2003) *Brandchild*, Kogan Page.

10   Joyce M Wolbury and James Pokrywczynski (2001) 'A Psychological Analysis of Generation Y College Students', *Journal of Advertising Research,* Sept–Oct.

11   'Generation Y: marketing changes', *Business Week*, 15 February 1999.

12   Martin Lindstrom (2003) *Brandchild*, Kogan Page.

13   'Cool for Cash', *Marketing Week*, 15 August 2002.

14   'Generation Y: marketing changes', *Business Week*, 15 February 1999.

15   William Strauss (1991) *Generations: The History of America's Future*, McGraw-Hill.

16   Carol L. Cone *et al.* (2003) 'Cause and Effects', *Harvard Business Review*, July.

17   Chris Anderson (2000) 'The disaffected', from 'Bright Young Things: A Survey of the Young', *The Economist*, 23 December, p. 7.

18   'Generation Y: marketing changes', *Business Week*, 15 February 1999.

19   Future Foundation/NTS (1998) *BT/First Direct Survey*, Future Foundation.

20   Greater London Authority (2002) *Whatever Gets You Through the Night: 24 Licensing in London*, Greater London Authority, November, p. 7.

21   Murray Melbin (1987) *Night as Frontier*, Free Press.

22   Greater London Authority (2002) *Whatever Gets You Through the Night: 24 Licensing in London*, Greater London Authority, November.

23   Greater London Authority (2002) *Late-Night London: Planning and Managing the Late-Night Economy,* Greater London Authority, SDS Technical Report Six, June.

24   Chris Anderson (2000) 'Bright Young Things: A Survey of the Young', *The Economist*, 23 December.

25   Janet Wiscombe (2000) 'Layoffs hit younger workers', *Workforce*, March.

26   Ibid.

27   'Tomorrow's Child', *The Economist*, 23 December 2000.

4   INSIDE COOL

1   'Workplace', *Director*, April 2003, p. 36.

2   Chris Anderson (2000) 'Know Future', from 'Bright Young Things: A Survey of the Young', *The Economist*, 23 December.

3   Jod Mitchell (2003) 'Suddenly, life smells sweeter', *Daily Telegraph*.

4   Michel Syrett and Jean Lammiman (2002) *Successful Innovation: How to Encourage and Shape Profitable Ideas*, Economist Books.

5   Kenneth Labiche, *Fortune*, 1995.

6   'The big leap', *The Economist*, 15 January 2000, p. 17.

7   'How to manage a dream factory', *The Economist*, 18 January, p. 75.

8   Jean Lammiman and Michel Syrett (1998) 'Does your alma mater matter?' *MBA: The Magazine for Business Masters*, March, p. 39.

9   Chris Anderson (2000) 'The kids are all right', from 'Bright Young Things: A Survey of the Young', *The Economist*, 23 December, p. 4.

10 Michel Syrett and Jean Lammiman (1997) 'Britain's own tiger economy', *Director*, January, p. 33.

11 Jean Lammiman and Michel Syrett (1998) *Innovation at The Top: Where Directors Get Their Ideas From*, Roffey Park Institute, September.

12 Sumantra Goshal and Christopher Bartlett (1998) *The Individualised Corporation*, William Heinemann, Random House.

13 Denise Rousseau (1998) *Psychological Contracts in Organisations: Understanding Written and Unwritten Agreement*, Sage.

14 Michel Syrett and Jean Lammiman (1999) 'Forget IQ: it's brains that matter', *The Observer*, 7 November.

15 Ibid.

16 Alex Osborne (1995) *Creative Imagination*, Charles Scribner.

17 Tom Kelley with Jonathan Littman (2001) *The Art of Innovation: Lessons in Creativity from IDEO, America's Leading Design Firm*, Doubleday/Currency.

18 Andy Smith and Annette Sinclair (2003) *What Makes an Excellent Virtual Manager?* Roffey Park Institute, April.

19 Jean Lammiman and Michel Syrett (2000) *Entering Tiger Country: How Ideas are Shaped in Organisations*, Roffey Park Institute, November.

20 'Generation Y: the graduates who dare to ask for more', *The Times*, Appointments section, 17 April 2003, p. 2.

21 Cathy Sheehan, Peter Holland and Robert Hecker (2002) *Organisational change and the psychological contract*, University of Tasmania School of Management.

22 Michel Syrett and Jean Lammiman (2000) 'Happily Landed: British Airways and Innovation', *People Management*, 28 September, pp. 24–30.

23 Ricardo Semler (2003) *The Seven Day Weekend*, Century.

24 R.B. Gallupe and W.H. Cooper (1993) 'Brainstorming electronically', *Sloan Management Review*, No. 4.

25 Michel Syrett and Jean Lammiman (1999) *Management Development: Making the Investment Count*, Economist Books, pp. 160–61.

26 Jean Lammiman and Michel Syrett (2000) *Entering Tiger Country: How Ideas are Shaped in Organisations*, Roffey Park Institute, November.

27 Johaan Roos (1996) 'Intellectual capital: what you can measure, you can manage', *Perspectives for Managers*, No. 10, November.
28 Gordon Shaw *et al.* (1998) 'Strategy stories: how 3M is rewriting business planning', *Harvard Business Review*, May–June.

5 CRUX

1 'Today, son, all of this is yours', *The Economist*, 23 December 2000, p. 89.
2 Ibid, p. 90.
3 Ibid, p. 89.
4 Robert Cooper (1998) 'No longer out of the barrel of a gun', *MBA: The Magazine for Business Masters*, January, pp. 5–10.
5 Michel Syrett and Klari Kingston (1995) 'GE's Hungarian Light Switch', *Management Today*, April.
6 'In a spin', *The Economist*, 1 March 2003, p. 66.
7 Shafik Meghji (2003) 'Music fans who download free songs may be sued in net piracy clampdown', *Evening Standard*.
8 'Upbeat', *The Economist*, 1 November 2003, p. 76.
9 Amy Kover (2000) 'The Hot Idea of the Year', *Fortune*, 26 June, p. 61.
10 Michel Syrett (1996) 'Nurturing ideas pays dividends', *Asian Business*, February.
11 'An end to slavery', *The Economist*, 24 November 2001, p. 76.
12 The Industrial Society (now the Work Foundation) Case Study on Nortel Networks, Report No. 88, *Managing Innovation*, p. 26.
13 Martin Lindstrom (2003) *Brandchild*, Kogan Page.
14 'A full life', *The Economist*, 4 September 1999, p. 91.
15 Michel Syrett and Jean Lammiman (2000) 'Happily Landed: British Airways and Innovation', *People Management*, 28 September.
16 Leon Kreitzman (1999) *The 24 Hour Society*, Profile Books.
17 Charles Cumming (1997) 'Is anyone still laughing?' *The Daily Telegraph*, 22 May.
18 Ron Zempke, Claire Raines and Bob Filipczak (2001) *Generations at Work: Managing the Clash of Veterans, Boomers, Xers and Nexters in Your Workplace*, Amacom.

6 COOL LEADERSHIP

1 Carol Kennedy (2001) *The Next Big Idea: Managing in the Digital Economy*, Random House, p. 169.
2 Jane Simms (2002) 'Young, free and single-minded', *Director*, June, p. 56.

3   Jean Lammiman and Michel Syrett (1998) *Innovation at The Top: Where Directors Get Their Ideas From*, Roffey Park Institute, September.
4   Ibid.
5   Leadership column, *Director*, April 2003, p. 36.
6   Anna Foster (1988) 'Virgin's New-Found Modesty', *Management Today*, March.
7   Leadership column, *Director*, April 2003.
8   *The Times,* 4 April, 2003.
9   Leadership column, *Director*, April 2003.

7   MANAGING COOL

1   Jean Lammiman and Michel Syrett (2000) *Entering Tiger Country: How Ideas are Shaped in Organisations*, Roffey Park Institute, November.
2   Lecture subsequently published in Anthony Jay (1987) *Management and Machiavelli: Power and Authority in Business Life*, Random Century.
3   Michel Syrett and Jean Lammiman (2001) *Creativity*, Capstone, ExpressExec series.
4   Clive Shepherd (2002) 'The DNA of an e-tutor, *IT Training*, November, p. 26.
5   Michel Syrett and Jean Lammiman (2002) *Management Development*, Capstone, ExpressExec series.
6   Michel Syrett and Jean Lammiman (1999) *Management Development; Making the Investment Count*, Economist Books.
7   Adapted from guidelines published in Ron Zempke, Claire Raines and Bob Filipczak (2000) *Generations at Work: Managing the Clash of Veterans, Boomers, Xers and Nexters in Your Workplace*, Amacom.
8   Profiles adapted from interviews published in Dimitry Elias Legar (2000) 'Help, I'm the New Boss', *Fortune*, 29 May, pp. 85–7.
9   Bruce Tulgan (2001) *Managing Generation Y*, HRD Press.

8   BRAINSTORMING COOL

1   R.B. Gallupe and W.H. Cooper (1993) 'Brainstorming electronically', *Sloan Management Review*, No. 4.
2   Tom Kelley with Jonathan Littman (2001) *The Art of Innovation: Lessons in Creativity from IDEO, America's Leading Design Firm*, Doubleday/Currency.

INDEX

advertising 35–6, 38, 45–6, 66, 213–14
Ahmed, Ajaz 162–4
Ahmed, Shami 166–70
AKQA 162–4
Alexander, Chloe 93–4
Allan, Andy 156
Allan, David 106–7
W H Allen 174
Amazon.com 53
Anderson, Chris 7
AOL (America Online) 97–8
architecture 79–80
attitudes 49–50, 226–7
Avon 71
awareness 90, 217–18, 224
    cause branding 70–72
    cynical 68–70
    practical 70
    social policy 72–4

baby boomers 5, 34, 47, 61, 62, 86, 87, 93
balance *see* work-life balance
Bannister, Matthew 177
Barcelona 79, 83
Beckham, David 47
Beinhart, Peter 197–8
Bells 219
Billingsley, Gene 56
Blair, Tony 67
boo.com 7, 174–5
Bowie, David 141, 142
Brady Chris 101–4
brainstorming 114–15, 121–2, 125
    day dreaming 210
    dos/don'ts 207–8
    five steps 205–6
    humour 201–2
    ideal if 208–9
    language 199–200
    metaphor 209

in practice 203–8
remote 202–3
reverse 208, 210
suggested approach 206–7
techniques 208–11
wildest ideas 211
brand/s 35, 212
    awareness 64–5, 217–18
    cause branding 70–72
    and children 64–5
    as cool 68
    customer point of view 163
    distinctiveness of 164–5
    establishing value/exploiting
        equity 173
    generational differences 152–3
    humour/language 214–16
    image/targeting 167
    interactive worlds 213–14
    24/7 living 218–20
    loyalty 65–7
    media link-ups 164
Branson, Richard 7, 173–4, 176, 178–9
Brewster, Chris 99
bridge jobs 153–4
British Airways (BA) 62, 79–80, 116, 119, 154–6, 182
British Petroleum (BP) 215
British Satellite Broadcasting (BSB) 174
Buck, Pearl S. 84
Buckingham, Jane 37
Buffy the Vampire Slayer 11, 37, 38, 42
Buller, Caroline 99, 181
business skills 20
Business Ventures Group 106
Business Week 86
Butterfield, Jeremy 40
Buybuddy.com 178
Byron, Chris 116, 189–90

cafe society 80
Caffe Nero 165, 166
Calvin, William 128
Capitol Radio 175
career development 117–18
career/work attitudes
    conventional/unconventional 22
    cynicism/disillusionment 24–8,
        32–3
    loyalty to company 23–4
    negative 30
    safety/security 21, 23, 32
    shaping 30–31
Case, Steve 97
Centre for Advanced Spatial
        Analysis (London University
        College) 82–3
Channel Four 185
Channelware 107
Chartered Institute of Personnel and
        Development 12
Chernin, Peter 98
child labour 134–7
Cobb, Ron 34
Coffee Republic 164–6
communication 115–16, 121–4
computer games 34–7
Comscore Media Metrix 142
ConAgra Foods 71, 72
Conducent 214
Cone 71–2
Converse 48–9
Cooper, Robert 138
Copenhagen 79, 83
corporate/social policy 70–74
cosmetics 146–8
counterfeit goods 142–3
Coupland, Douglas 25–6
Cranfield School of Management 99
CSIRO 118
24/7 culture 77, 79–84, 104, 120,
        218–20

De Bono, Edward 113
Devereux, Robert 173
Diageo 219
diffusion research 50–51
Draper, Simon 173–4
Dugdale, Keith 117

The Economist 7, 15, 73, 86, 88
Eddington, Rod 155
Electronic Frontier Foundation 145
email 124–6, 192–5

employment 225–6
    accommodate employee
        differences 157
    anywhere/anytime 77
    atmosphere 92
    challenge/astonish 99–100
    create workplace choices 157
    employer/employee connection
        105
    environment 94–9
    family friendly 76
    female 76
    generational differences 151–6
    legislation 75
    long-hours culture 77, 79–84
    motivation/mental engagement
        99–100, 170–72
    new patterns 75–6
    operate from sophisticated
        management style 158
    respect competence/initiative
        158
enfantreprenurs 7
entrepreneurs 9, 227–8
    case studies 162–79
environment 136
    career management 117–18
    flexible 118–24
    virtual 119–24
    work/leisure combination
        119–21
Epcot Centre 197
Evans, Chris 175–7

Fast Company 99–100, 112
Feeding Children Better 71
Filipczak, Bob 157
Five Forces Model (Porter) 19
Fizz 19–20
Forrester Research 214
Frank, Thomas 45
Friday, Angus 4–5, 18–20
Fritzche, Yvonne 7
Furdyk, Micael 178
Future Foundation 156

games industry 56–60
Gates, Bill 4
General Electric (GE) 23, 137–40
Generation X 5, 11, 16, 25, 34, 38,
        47, 61, 62, 86, 87, 93, 119, 212
Generation Y see Millenials
generational differences
    accommodate 157

branding 152–3
changing employment patterns
    151–6
language/humour 156–7
recruitment/retention 153, 158
similarities 153, 154
Germany 88
Gibson, William 41
Giger, H.R. 34
Ginger Media group 175–6
Gladwell, Malcolm 48, 51
globalism 73, 135
GMT 56
Goldman Sachs 23
Gordon, Dee Dee 48
Goshal, Sumantra 20, 104–5
Grokster 145

Hartley, L.P. 5
Hashemi, Bobby and Sahar 164–6
Hawkins, Peter 193
Hayman, Michael 178
Hayward, Martin 49
HBO 98–9
Henley Centre/Management
    College 13, 49, 122
Higgs, Malcolm 13
Hilfiger, Tommy 65–6, 152, 212
Hoberman, Brent 4, 7
home-working 28, 108, 120
Huang, Henry 14
humour 42–4, 74–5, 109, 156–7,
    201–2, 214–16

IBM 153
    SkillTeam (IBM) 153
icons/iconology 33
    ability to shape own worlds 34–7
    loyalty to your own 37–8
Idealab 106
ideas/creativity
    challenging 181–3
    freedom 145
    generating/spotting 130
    inspired/fostered 144–9
    mental images 100–102
    negative experiences 108–11
    outside of work 104, 120
    science/art combination 102–4
    technology 111–12
    third place source 105–8
    turning on the switch 100–112
    see also intellectual property
        rights

IDEO 116, 203–5
IKEA 215–16
Intellectual Property Awards and
    Recognition Plan 149–51
    cumulative awards 150
    patent filing 150
    patent issuance 150
    significant patent awards 150
intellectual property rights
    awards/recognition 149–51
    ownership issues 144–9
    piracy/plagiarism 140–44
    see also ideas/creativity
International Institute for
    Management Development
    (IMD) 127
International Monetary Fund (IMF)
    73
Internet 6, 11, 39, 124–6, 213
    customer dialogue 56
    richness vs easy access 53–5
    transactions on 52–6
intimacy 89–90, 223
    commercial 52–60
    global 52
    local 51–2
intranet 55, 124–7, 131
IQdos 185

Jackson, Michael 141, 142
Jackson, Peter 34
Japan 87–8
Jay, Anthony 183
job security 21, 23, 32, 93, 95, 105
Joe Bloggs 166–70

KaZaA 141–2
Kelley, David 114, 204–5
Kelley, Tom 204
Kendall Tarrant Worldwide 13
Kielberger, Craig 132, 134
King, Ros 118
KMA 185
KPMG 117

La passeggiata 79, 80
Ladenburg Thalmann & Co 74
Lambert, Rachel 194
Lane Fox, Martha 7
language 19–200, 38–42, 47, 125–30,
    156–7, 214–16
Lanier, Jaron 124
Lank, Thomas 152
Larose, Gord 106–7

lastminute.com 7, 53
leadership 227–8
  asking why questions 178, 179
  broad range of interests 172
  case histories 162–79
  decision-making 161
  delegation 165, 173–4
  knowledge of market 168–70
  limitations/strengths 162
  professional management 163
  role of 179
  transparent/open 172
  worker-friendly 171–2
Leander, Kajsa 7, 174
Lennon, John 141
Levi's 66, 152–3, 212
life criteria
  friends 37–8
  quality of 20–22
  social aspects 22, 37
  work flexibility 22–3
Limelight Promotions 18
Lindstrom, Martin 35, 66, 152, 199
Lohmann, Fred von 145
London 79–84, 219
Lord of the Rings 35, 37, 98, 213
loyalty 60–67, 90, 188, 223–4
  brand 64–7
  corporate 70–72
  self-made community 61, 63–4
  workplace 61–4
Lucozade 213–14

McCartney, Paul 141
McDonald's 153
McDougall, Carrie 133
MacGowan, Rodger B. 56–60
MacInnes, Bruce 193–5
McKie, Rod 165
McLuhan, Marshall 68
Madeley, Richard 47
management 227
  continuous coaching 183–7
  creative challenging 181–2
  election by subordinates 171
  millennials as 195–8
  professional 163
  quality of 180
  style 158, 168
  team-building 188–90
  virtual teamworking 190–95
Manchester 80, 83
Manfrey, Barbara 176
Marketing Week 67

Massachusetts Institute of
  Technology (MIT) 202
Mead, Margaret 6–7
Melbin, Murray 82
mergers/acquisitions 23–4, 95–9
metrosexual 50
Microsoft 178
Millennials 4
  characteristics 12–15, 195
  cynicism of 66–7
  demand respect 9
  description of 6
  entrepreneurial 9
  formative influences 44, 222
  independent 9
  opportunities 196
  origins 221–2
  outlook 10–11
  response 196–7
  social networks/connectivity of
    11–12, 15
  technologically knowledgeable
    6–7
  think differently 8
  threats 196
  vulnerability of 10
  want opportunity more than
    money/security 9
  welcome change 7
Morgan, Robert 152
Moroshima, Motohiro 88
Morpheus 145
motivation 88–100, 170–72, 191
Munkster 144
Murdoch, Rupert 98
music industry 140–42, 143–4, 145

Nakamura, Shuji 148–9
Napster 140–41, 144, 145, 146
NeoPets.com 35–6, 67, 214
networking 169
new economy 53
The New Republic 197
Nichia Corporation 148–9
night life 80–84
Nike 74, 163
Noon, G.K. 101–2, 166
Nortel Networks 106–8, 149–51
Northridge, Tamsin 14

O'Bannon, Dan 34
Ontario Secondary School Students'
  Association 133
Opinion Research Council 7

Osborne, Alex 113
out of box thinking 113–14, 178

Palczynski, James R. 74
part-time work 28, 108
J.C. Penney & Co. 215
Pennywise 166
PepsiCo 69
Perrin, Towers 9
Petrie, Doug 38
Piper, Billie 177
Porter, Michael 19
Prêt-à-Manger 165
PriceWaterhouseCoopers 24, 111–12
Procter & Gamble 23–4
public policy
    child labour 134–7
    multinational interests vs local
        sensibilities 137–40
    UN agenda 137
    youth engagement 132–4

Quart, Alison 64–5
Quinn, Joseph 153

Raines, Claire 85, 157
Rank Xerox 62
Reagan, Margaret 9
Recording Industry Association of
    America (RIAA) 145, 146
report writing 128–9, 131
Ridderstråle, Jonas 17
risk 91, 224–5
    attitude to 84–5
    and the better life 85–6
    cultural aspects 88–9
    social uncertainties 86–8
Robertso, Sheila 185
Roddick, Anita 7
Roffey Park Management Institute
    11, 100, 115, 116, 125, 181
Roos, Johaan 127
Roper Youth Report 85
Rousseau, Denise 105
Royal College of Art (RCA) 102
Royal Mail 110

St Barnardo's 187
Salama, Eric 53
Saloner, Garth 161, 177
Salzman, Marian 47–8, 50, 69, 70
San Francisco 83
Sanders & Sidney 61
Save the Children 182, 192–5

science fiction 34, 213
Scott, Ridley 34
Seattle Coffee Company 165
Semco 92, 119, 170–72
Semler, Ricardo 92, 113, 119–20,
    170–72, 178
Shaw, Gordon 128
Sheehan, Cathy 118
Shimada, Norika 146–8
Shin, Susan 197
Shiseido 146–8
Silsbee, Peter 85
Sinclair, Annette 115
Smith, Andy 115, 190
Smith, J. Walker 68–9
social infrastructure 63
social policy, international
    corporate 136–40
Spangler, David 66
spin-off ventures 105–6
Standard Chartered Bank 122
Starbucks 165, 166
Steir, Merle 46, 50, 64
Strathclyde Business School 19
Strauss, William 69
Sugar, Alan 7
Sullivan, John 156
Sutton, Robert 130
Swords, Dominic 123, 124

3M 128
Tapscott, Don 6
team building
    characteristic 188
    example 189–90
    opportunity 188
    response 188
    threat 188
teamwork 114–15, 116
    virtual 190–95
time users
    convenience driven 78
    fast-laners 77, 78, 156
    past-timers 78, 156
    pressured conservatives 78
Time Warner 97, 98
Tomb Raider 35, 37, 213
Torp, Niels 79
TransAtlantic Ventures 20
transport 81–2, 219
trend-spotting 46–51
Tucker, Jenny 186
Tulgan, Bruce 9, 86, 93, 198
Tungsram 137–40

tweenagers 35

UCLA 96
United Nations (UN) 133, 137
    guidelines on international
        investment 138
University of Tasmania 118
urban living 79–84

van der Heijden, Kees 19
Vanity Fair 7
Verizon 145
Video Arts 183
Virgin group 102, 174, 175–6, 177
virtual teamworking 190
    characteristic 191
    example 192–5
    opportunity 191
    response 191
    threat 191

Warner Brothers 98
Waterside 79–80
Wellington (New Zealand) 133–4
Willmott, Michael 77, 156
work management
    brainstorming 114–15
    out of box thinking 113–14

team leadership 116–17
    traditional 112–13
    virtual 115
work–life balance 91, 224
    24/7 culture 77, 79–84
    origins 75–7
World Trade Organization (WTO)
    73, 135
WPP 53

Yankelovich Partners Inc 69
Young & Rubicon 70
youth
    changing outlook 9–16
    as consumers/entrepreneurs
        4–5, 9
    corporate understanding of
        16–17
    economic power 46–7
    new generation 5–7
    rebel culture 45
    surveys on 7–9, 13–14
    thinking/behaving 3–4
    see also Millennials
Youth Concepts 46

Zempke, Ron 157
Zohar, Danah 111–12